Made in Marmaris

The Marmaris Diaries

Louise Bell

Other titles in The Marmaris Diaries:

Book 1: The Final Summer of Vodka

Book 1.5: Back in Blighty

Book 2: Once Upon a Whisky

All available on Amazon

Parental Advisory - Explicit Content

Not for the easily offended. I swear. Quite a lot.

Copyright © 2018 Louise Bell

All rights reserved.

ISBN: 1721932038
ISBN-13: 978-1721932030

DEDICATION

For Sister.
They say that friends are the family we choose for ourselves, and Sister, you were the best friend a gal could have. Till we meet again in the windy city.

And not forgetting Gucci, because well, the little sod deserves it.

CONTENTS

	Acknowledgments	i
1	Chapter 1	1
2	Chapter 2	22
3	Chapter 3	54
4	Chapter 4	82
5	Chapter 5	98
6	Chapter 6	104
7	Chapter 7	113
8	About the Author	126
9	Plea from the Author	127

ACKNOWLEDGMENTS

A huge big thank you to Karen and Dan for providing their keen eye and thoughts on not just the book, but the cover also.
Thank you to the ex-pats of Marmaris because your character inspiration knows no limits.
And finally, thank you Mum and Dad. Without you both, The Marmaris Diaries wouldn't exist. That doesn't mean you're allowed to read them though…

JULY

Thursday 20th, 2017
Current Location: The Parents Gaff, Manchester
Time: 20.30pm
Weight: 73.5 Kilos. I kid you fucking not.

Dear Diary,

If you are picking this up for the very first time, might I warn you that it belongs to me, Lei Lawson, and me, Lei, can be described as the following:
- A socially awkward kinda gal until copious amounts of vodka and/or whisky have been consumed
- A party animal that loves to curse
- A 36-year-old married pregnant vegetarian, that is struggling to see the bad side of eating for two

What a cunt – and by cunt, I mean fat cunt - and by fat cunt, I mean me – the beached whale sitting on my Mum and Dad's sofa writing this.

I did warn you that I like to curse. The question is, have I offended you yet?

If so, may I suggest that you put this down and carry on with your day. After all, this is someone's diary you are reading.
However, should you find yourself part of my club – and you know the one I mean - you are welcome to read on, preferably whilst sipping a vodka cocktail.

Oh hey there! You stayed!
Welcome to the cunts club my friend.

So, let's get down to business;
I decided to start another diary for a couple of reasons:
-Reason 1: I am only going to be pregnant once, so I figured that when I am old and grey and quite possibly senile, it may be an interesting read to see how the last three months of this experience went - should I happen to forget.
-Reason 2: I'm bored.

As per all my other diaries, this one too has a goal.
I'm going for the obvious since I dare not tempt fate, and thus, this diaries goal is to have a happy healthy baby with a name that I adore. The name part is proving harder than I originally thought, what with Husbando Barış vetoing literally everything... Mo fo.
Oh, and I also wish to be rich and famous and live in my dream home with a nanny, walk in wardrobe, swimming pool, and a massive garden for Gucci with a marquee where I can hold garden parties and gigs with live bands, plus a garage the size of a small village for my Mini Countryman, Jeep and fleet of various other cars.

I like to aim high!

But enough of that chatter. Instead let me bring you up to speed with life right now:

Although I still live in Marmaris, I happen to be back in Blighty on my annual mid-season escape from the sun. It's raining and the conservatory's leaking. Not much changes in these 'ere parts, except this time visiting I'm 6 months pregnant and the size of Oldham. Yup, ole preggers over here is feeling less wannabe socialite and more absolute 'obeast', but do 'ya know what? It's all good. Life has turned out exactly as I planned, and this Marmaris lover couldn't be any bloody happier.

Really?
Well no, not quite...

You could say that life has been eventful these past few months.
I mean, when is it not in the life of Lei?

Since March, when I finished my last diary instalment, there have been a couple of noticeable occurrences:
-Occurrence 1: I finally deleted Lorraine from Facebook (Yippee ki-yay kemosabe)! I mean who needs a 65-year-old attention seeker in one's life when one is preparing to give birth?
Not this prenatal female.
I've enough going on with without her need to outdo me being thrown in the mix. I mean the last thing I want is someone telling me how fabulous *they* looked when up the duff, when I know that fabulous is the last thing that *I* look.

-Occurrence 2: I have lost Lacie to an Italian yacht owning sugar daddy. Yup, as we speak, Lacie is currently living the high life cruising the Italian Riviera. I kid you not, she has only gone and landed herself a multi-millionaire.
That girl always was destined for riches, even if they aren't her own...

But oh, how I miss my best friend. Especially since my dear ole (Mr) Sister died.
You remember Sister, don't you? My non-blood relative that was like family to me.
He left us just over a month ago and I can't think of him without a breaking into floods.
Like now - my face is soaking wet with the mention of his name.

He passed whilst repping in Portugal. I suppose there are worse places to die, but I can't think of any right now…

My GBF Anthony called to tell me the news. I was home at the time, watching the Grenfell Towers burn to buggery, already shrouded in an overwhelming amount of sadness.
Thank God it was Anthony that called and no one else because my reaction was horrific. It started with silence, escalated to screaming and ended in sobbing. Quite possibly the saddest sobs you have ever heard.

We knew Sister had been admitted to hospital, but not one of us thought it would end this way. Poor bugger had only just arrived to start work for the season too, all filled with energy, hope and wonder, just like the start of any new season.
Alas, it wasn't to be, and his time was up when he suffered the second stroke within a few short months…
Its seems like yesterday when Anthony introduced Sister and I during the summer of '05 back when we were lowly Marmaris reps. At the time they were quite the item. I say item when I really mean Sister was the long-suffering partner of Anthony, a guy that can sometimes be an arsehole to be in a relationship with, yet non the less, I love him dearly.
From there on in we were known as the 3 amigos, or, as the management team liked to call us, cunt 1, 2 and 3.

Anthony eventually moved on to repping pastures new, leaving Sister and I as the gruesome twosome. We went on to go through some ridiculous situations together, including the horrific break-up of the dreaded ex. Had it not of been for dear ole Sister, I'm not sure I would have made it through that shit part of life.

Let me tell you about this one time that we ended up in a Marmaris brothel, right in the heart of the bazaar. Before you think it, we weren't there to earn a couple of quid, only to visit a friend of Sisters, although given the state of the game I think we would have cleaned up.

It was during the thick of my break-up, and Sister thought he could cheer me up with showing me that life could be worse; I could be a lady-boy prozzie that sold my tat in a rent a room by the hour type of stinking shit hole establishment.

Murat, Sister's *friend*, was ever so forthcoming in making us feel welcome and introducing us to the 'girls'. He went out of his way to lighten my shitty mood, and I swear I very nearly left there with a smile on my face from the ludicrous scenario, all until Murat asked me how I was *really*, and I burst out crying (3 seconds after laughing). One of the lady-boys offered me what I thought to be a hanky and I took it gratefully to mop up my sodden face. It was only when I got home I found it to be a pair of women's used panties covered in what I believe to be shit stains. Could have been blood - either way it was fucking gross.

Jesus, I couldn't pick Sister up off the floor for laughter. We cried 'till our nether regions shed tears.

And that 'Dear Diary', was a good day. One of the thousands of Sister memories that I am lucky enough to have.

In actual fact, I could write a book with all of our shenanigans. Maybe one day, I will.

It is, however, high time that I stopped eluding my grief so that I can begin to move on. Not from Sister of course as he will always be with me, but from this awful state of mind that simply wont budge. Yup, it's safe to say that I've been grief dodging since he departed, yet I know it must be confronted for the fog to lift.
The time, 'Dear Diary', is now.

Let me warn you that the following couple of lines will not be of the usual brand of sarcastic sunshine that I mostly dish up, because after all, we are talking about my dead best friend here.

So, here's what needs to come out:

Firstly, I feel numb – fucking numb. Like it's not really happened, but actually it has because I have no way of contacting Sister to ask if it's real because the mo fo 'aint replying to my FB messages these days.

Secondly, I feel angry – really fucking angry. I mean WTF, who seriously thought it would be a good idea to call Sister to his next destination when I'm clearly not ready to join him?
And why him?
Why not some rapist or murderer that no one would miss?

Thirdly, I feel confused – dazed and confused. One day I'm good, quite positive really, my mood is high and I even find myself laughing at the crazy fond memories - and the next, I'm down in the depths of hell with not even booze as a crutch due to being up the duff.
Sometimes life is not so beautiful...

Fourthly, I feel somewhat in denial. Like no. Just no.
I wake up in the morning, and for the briefest of moments all is well with the world. That beautiful period lasts approximately 5.5 seconds before memory kicks in and tears start streaming.
Yet somehow, as well as being upset, I also don't feel like he has 'gone' just yet. Maybe not enough time has passed then eh?
Mind you, he might very well be here with me as he told me a long time back that if he went first he would come back to haunt me. Fucker said he would wait 'till I was nicely asleep then sit on the end of my bed and stare at me till I woke up and proceed to scare the living Bejesus out of me. That's nice isn't it?
Actually, it's surprisingly comforting knowing that he may be popping in from time to time. Sometimes I catch Guch staring into thin air or running
over to a corner in the sitting room in excitement, and it just makes me wonder.

Guch always did have a special bond with Sister. After all, we pretty much raised him together.
In fact, it was Anthony and Sister that convinced me that Gucci was my soul mutt one drunken day in the pet shop, and they were right too.

FFS I woke up the next morning and near shit myself when I saw this cute little puppy asleep quite soundly with his head next to mine...

Sister, Guch and I went on to become an odd little family that constantly seemed to get into trouble. Trouble of the good sort. Trouble that makes you piss your pants in laughter and you thank your lucky stars that you have a little ole family like this.

By Christ how I miss him.

I suppose I'm lucky because I have a great imagination and all I need to do is close my eyes and I can see Sisters goofy grin. Sometimes I have conversations with him too - honest to God, full-blown conversations.
In my mind, he is now the spirit version of Google, so I tend to ask him the same type of things that I would should we be sat opposite each other. Things like 'is it true that when you fart you inhale shit particles', or 'what excuse can I use for not wanting sex this time?'.
I bet you're wondering if I ever get a reply?
Yes, when I actually consult Google, who I now fully believe to be Sister, I most certainly do.

He would have been God Father you know, not that I got the chance to tell him.
Now all the plans we made for winter have been replaced with a big black hole of emptiness, and damn that Sister with his sheer absence from my life!

Anyway, that's quite enough of that. It's time to bring about something lighter before I slip into the labyrinth of doom. Something else Sister and I did every hangover Sunday...

You will be happy to hear that things have been rather solid with ole Husbado. We've had no major arguments, no fall outs and no silent weeks. Yup, all's going swimmingly in that department. This is quite

possibly because for the last 5.5 months I've been sober as a judge and not aggravating him with my pissed-up ways.
Bloody hell fire, maybe all that crap really was my boozy fault?
Ahh fuck it, no use in crying over spilt vodka, what's done is done and when I've dropped this sprog normal service will resume just as soon the drinking does.

Now that my belly's popped I think it's finally dawned on us both that this shit's real and we're going to have a baby.
A fucking baby I tell you!
I was so obsessed with getting knocked up that I don't think I ever really gave much thought to what was going to happen once I was. Put it this way – I have bought sod all baby related because I have 100% been living in la la land. It's only now that I'm getting bigger (and no longer simply looking fat) that I realised I need to gear this up a notch. The nursery is not going to create itself and stuff isn't going to magically appear once the baby does.
Unlike Lacie, I don't live in a fairy tale.

But wouldn't you think with all the gifts I've received that it may just excite me into buying more for my soon to arrive little human?
It hasn't.
This is totally out of character for a self-confessed shopaholic, so I have to ask, what's a girl to do when one simply can't force oneself to pull one's lazy finger out?

Come to Blighty – that's what!

Near enough upon touchdown Mum gave me a stern talking to and yanked my lazy finger so hard that I doubt I will ever be able to pick my nose with it ever again.
Proverbially speaking off course…

Those proverbial's caused a result (finally) because guess what I did today? Went baby shopping, that's what - and in my all-time fave shop Primark too!

As I literally had no idea what I was doing and clearly needed expert help, I roped my UK bestie Hannah into the shopping madness. She was a God send in what I can only describe as a mine field of baby bombs.
FML, who knew babies needed so much stuff?!
Vests to wear under baby grows, mittens, some sort of weird religious cloth that does 101 jobs - and that's just the start of it!

It's a girl by the way, in case you were wondering.
But this 'ere Mother to be doesn't do girly shit, oh hells to the no. I am totally hoping that she will slide out a kick arse little hipster rock chick, that will one day rule the world.

As you can see, I still suffer from delusions that I will be raising a prophet. Who knows, maybe they won't be delusions at all? Maybe my little ninja will be the one to save us all. After all, it's about fucking time that someone did.

But I do miss boozing.
I was told that I would be so sick that the thought of drink wouldn't cross my mind. Well that hasn't happened, and still, even at 6 months pregnant, I want to get my drink on.
Before you raise that perfectly plucked brow, please know that I don't. I just want to. A lot.

Don't get me wrong 'Dear Diary', I am quite thankful that I've had a nice easy pregnancy to date, and I totally believe that I am one of the luckiest females to walk this planet what with having no morning sickness, dizziness or ludicrous cravings.
But what is it *they* say? Easy pregnancy, difficult birth?
Pa! I'll show *them*!
Whoever *they* are clearly don't know who I am now do they? If they did, they certainly wouldn't be suggesting such shite as they would know that it would freak me out, and now I'm going to obsess and Sister Google difficult bloody births.

Oh bollocks, and so it begins…

I have had pregnancy signs of course, my first being when baby Stella kicked at week 19. That was a funny experience let me tell you. Maternal is a foreign feeling to me, so when I felt baby Iris kick I was nearly sick. I'm getting used to it now, but I still don't find the feeling of baby Mia swinging around on my intestines as pleasurable as my best friend Sister G would have me believe.

Unfortunately, Barış is yet to feel her kick. Gucci on the other hand, lies with his furry little head on my tummy and when he feels baby Starr giving it some welly he opens his eyes and I swear he grins.

Yup, I think Guch has big brother syndrome and I couldn't be prouder.
In fact, I believe he knows exactly what's going on in my ever-protruding pot belly because:
-1: He's a clever little sod
-And 2: He has started to behave, which he has never done in the whole 12 years he has been on planet Earth.

No more pulling and/or dragging me down the street, no more rebellious behaviour and no more guzzling cat shit while out on our walks (him not me, obviously).
It's a different story entirely when he's around Barış, but, that's none of my business. All I know is that Gucci is a little diamond with me and I can't wait for him to meet baby Adeline.

And, that's just where I'm going to leave it for tonight.
I'm going to hit up Sister G while the naming mood takes me and see what other random shite pops out.
Then I'm going to eat half a chocolate cake. Not because I'm eating for two (because we all know that's a pile of crap), simply because I'm a greedy cunt and I can.

Cunt count: About 9?
And if you don't like that word, then what sort of unlucky one are you ;)

Tuesday, 25th July 2017
2nd Trimester, Week 26
Current Location: The Parents Gaff, Manchester
Time: 17.48pm

Dear Doom,

OK, so forget what I said about not even knowing I'm pregnant because FML – hello hormones, you vicious little bastards you!

I suppose one could say that I've done well so far, and all good things must come to an end.
I say fuck that shit! I neither want nor need to rock this pregnancy boat!

Yes, I am aware that I'm a late starter what with being only 2 weeks away from entering my 3rd trimester, but really, is there any need for things to change now?
Come on Lawson – don't let the final month's blow what has been a bloody marvellous pregnancy to date!

Today, I find myself totally out of sorts, and feel, well, blaaaaaa. Just so we're all on the same page and there's no confusion, blaaaa means: a big bag of stinkin' sweaty bollocks that have been left unwashed after sex.
Yup, I feel pretty damn grim right now.
Surly this can't all be down to pregnancy hormones, can it?

It doesn't help that I literally hate everyone, and I miss my boi Guch.

One minute I'm high as a kite, as happy as can be, and the next I find that I've crashed and burned and locked myself in the bathroom in a blubbering mess.
To make matters worse, mirrors don't help because when looking at said blubbering mess of a fat face it sends me into a downward spiral at just how hard I fought *not* to have a fat bloody face.
And scales should be banned too when pregnant, as while locked in the bathroom crying one's eyes out, it's simply too tempting not to jump on and check the damage.

Bollocks, I'm nearly 11 and a half stone! WT Actual F Man!

Clearly all my hard work of trying not to eat for 2 turned to shit as soon as I got to this country.
Damn you beautiful British food, damn you!
And on top it all off, I believe that as well as hormones and grief running rife through my veins, that I also have a touch of UK syndrome too.

Definition of UK syndrome:
A weird anxiety type feeling churning around in the pit of one's stomach, resulting in a bad case of impending doom and the shits, that seems to linger on and on until one finally gets on the plane home.
And it happens every.sodding.time.

All I can tell you is this: I feel like a fish out of water, but with water surrounding my every turn because the rain has not let up since I got off the plane. Normally I enjoy UK weather especially when I first arrive, but this has been that loathsome continuous sheet of North Sea drizzle that is enough to depress even the most positive of souls.

So, that's what I'm dealing right now.
F'ing marvellous eh!

I sometimes wonder how I'd cope if I had to move back. It's a daunting prospect but one that's been doing the rounds since I got a baby girl bun in my oven. Unfortunately for me, Barış loved the UK, and since we were over in April he has been dropping hints left right and centre about a possible move.
I was shocked - honest to God I didn't think he would like it. Alas he did, and now he can't understand why I would want to live anywhere else.

Maybe it's me then?

I remember from a really young age that I would cut up holiday brochures of far flung places and stick them all around the edges of my dressing table mirror. I would stare at them day in day out imagining myself living in these countries, breaking free of mundane life.

My favourites to cut up were Japan, Turkey, Cyprus, Portugal and the States. Barr the States, I have worked/lived in each of those places and holidayed in America just a few years ago.

That right there is the law of attraction at its finest, not that I knew it back then…
I swear that shit works man, I'm living sodding proof. Just look at my dairies FFS! 'The Final Summer of Vodka' really was when I met my man, and 'Once Upon a Whisky' started out with one goal, to get preggers – and well, would you just look at me now…?!

Don't get me wrong here, I'm not walking around thinking that everything I touch turns to gold, because well, it doesn't. I totally believe we make our own luck, and I usually do, but when it comes to friends I just don't know what happens.
Now that I have lost Lacie, I'm starting to feel like the odd one out again - the girl that doesn't fit in to any particular group. Unfortunately, I'm finding it virtually impossible to locate my brand of cunty friend these days.
It's not an unfamiliar feeling and I'm pretty sure it dates back to my high school days, getting kicked out of one then having to start again in another, and at the age of 14, well, I don't need to tell you that making new friends was rough – especially when the new school girls formed their cliques 3 solid years previous.

And that 'Dear Diary' is where my hatred of cliques started.

Not that the new school girls were nasty to me, they welcomed me in, and to the popular gang too which was a turn up for the books considering I was one of the most unpopular in my previous school…

Other than my bad girl ways, I'm not entirely sure why they let me in if I'm honest?

They oozed cool, they were uber fashionista, and everyone wanted to be them. Then there was me with my caked-on powder trying to cover my shiny skin, my goth like fashion, and, I had no idea how to behave around them...
They must have liked my fringe then.
It started way back in the middle of my head and was a perfect greasy mess. But it played its part and covered up the plethora of teen acne underneath. Looking back, that fringe would be bang on trend right now. In fact, a few years back I decided to re-create my youth and had 'half-moon bangs' cut in.
Never again.
As much as it looked the business, the fringe was just too high maintenance for a 'put it on top of your head and go' type of gal that I am. The thing took an inordinate amount of care with its daily washing, and you simply cannot leave the house without styling it...
No wonder it looked the mess that it did back in high school, and no wonder I got called 'chip fat' and other such delights...
Aren't kid's cunts...!

Anyway, I went on to witnesses clique life at its finest and soon realised it wasn't for a socially awkward kinda gal like myself.
Now I avoid such cliques like the plague. Girls in large groups, especially those found living in Marmaris, can be fucking bitches, even in their forties... Take Larissa's gang for example, they all bitch about each other behind each other's back, then form a hard and frosty exterior when all together, going on to bitch about everyone that isn't in their clique as and when they run into them...
Exactly the same as school, just 25 years on... Cliques weren't for me then and aren't for me now.

Nope, I'm a gal that likes to keep her friends separate, and there is nothing wrong with that, right? I'm not a lone wolf, but it wouldn't take much with what's offered up in my holiday resort these days. Talk about sly mo fo's...

But, at least I feel like I belong. Mainly to Gucci, but where there's a piss infested fur baby monster, there's a home.

Shite, I totally digressed there didn't I!?
All I know is that UK syndrome is not a pleasant feeling to be stuck with and I wish it would piss off.

Actually, I wish Barış were here. He would make a great candidate to take it out on. Alas, the universe decided to take pity on his soul and save his sorry arse from the wrath of Lei this time.
Mind you, I do firmly believe that he deserves some of the blame for my shitty mood considering it's his sperm that caused this pregnancy PMS.
Lucky little fucker...

So, who's left to take it out on then? My olds?
Oh hells no, not just 'cos that would be a shits trick, but also because Mum has only just got out of hospital.
Did I not mention? Baby brain strikes again...

My poor ole Mum had a knee replacement operation the day after I arrived and only came home on Saturday.

You may wonder if I came back to help her recuperate?
The short answer to that is no because the op was scheduled to happen 2 months ago, and she was supposed to be well on the way to recovery by now and able to come baby shopping with me.
Spoilt Brat Alert
So, what I'm about to say is going to sound shockingly terrible and I'm fully aware of it, but it's my diary and they are only thoughts after all.
So instead of beating around the bush, I'm just going to say it – feel free to judge at will:

Usually when I come to the UK I don't have to lift a finger and all I need to do is enjoy reverting to my teenage years, so for fucks sake how unlucky am I that Mums op got rescheduled to now?
I mean, shouldn't this be my time?
Am I not supposed to be reaping the pregnancy benefits?

By Christ, I'm so not geared up to take on the role of house Mummy, prepare 3 meals a day and clean this damn bungalow - especially not to Mums standards.
And what's with Dad not even knowing how to open a tin of beans? Deary God, they like to make life difficult for this pregnant Mary that hates to be anywhere near a kitchen, don't they!

Now I find myself having to cook full on healthy meals daily - veg and all - as Mum won't have any of this 'frozen food malarkey' in *her* kitchen.

Seriously, what have I done to deserve this?!

I didn't leave hot sodding Turkey to do here what I did there! I'm 6 months pregnant for the love of God! I didn't sign up for this!

Nope, no being pregnancy spoilt for this brat and it's not fair I tell you!

Crap I am the voice of misery, aren't I? However today it simply can't be helped.
I know we all get days like this, especially big fat pregnant mamma jamma's like myself, alas, today I feel like the only one ever to feel so shite about oneself.

But, I must remember that it's certainly not Mums fault.

Anyway, I better go now. I'm being summoned to cook dinner.
Ahh fuck off healthy shit, tonight we're having Chinky.

Sunday, 30th July 2017
Week 27
Current Location: The Parents Gaff, Manchester
Time: 11.10am

Dear Pregnant nips from outer space,

Jesus, it's bloody early in the day for an entry from me! Usually at this time on a Sunday I'm ensconced on the sofa with a naughty Guch next to me watching 'Sunday Brunch' on Channel 4 while drinking tea and eating toast. And prior to pregnancy you could almost guarantee that it would be with my usual Sunday hangover.

Since arriving in the UK, I have been rudely awoken at 8am daily to tend to the breakfast ritual of the olds. I shouldn't moan, but this is simply not natural for a lazy sloth like me. And to make matters worse, the sight of porridge makes me gip!

Dad says it's all in preparation for what's to come in just 3 short month's, and the sly ole mo fo is treating it like he's doing me the favour – but, I know his game. He's milking this shit for as long as he can. Don't blame him really. He has been spoilt in life by Mum and if I could get out of doing all this for as long as possible then I suppose I bloody would too...!

Anyway, I am happy to report that the hormones seemed to have calmed down somewhat and I couldn't be more grateful. By Christ it's no fun being a raving loony, getting upset at just about everything.
Take a normal Facebook call to Baris for example. What would normally end in a good-natured bit of banter had me up a height and cursing him to hell and gone – all because he was at his friend's house and couldn't put Gucci on video chat.
I was livid, fucking livid.
And, I've not even apologised since because I'm still half convinced he did it on purpose... Although, the thought is there to do so eventually.

I better make a mental note to show him a nip or something the next time we video chat. Thankfully, a nip is usually enough to banish any negative thoughts on his part.
Gotta love a simple man with simple fixes.
Mind you, the state of my nipples at this present time is quite grotesque. They are alien like, all dark brown and minging, and happen to be the size of plates! Grim I tell you, just grim.
And what the hell is the weird crusty shit that has appeared on the nip tips?

Maybe not such a wise idea to show ole Husbando if even I'm freaked out by the state of them.
Poor bastard would get nightmares and blame them on me too!

May have to be a flash of the gash instead then.

So, what have I done to cheer myself up these last few days?
Well, the first thing to put a smile on my face was a second visit to Primark, but not for baby stuff this time.
My only pleasure in life is Gucci, booze and new clothes, so what with booze off the table and Gucci not here, one must make sure to get some treats in somewhere right? Baby on its way or not, this girl needs new threads.

God I love Primark!
I could literally spend all day in there, which I did on Wednesday. I came out with a renewed love for life and some solid peace of mind. Primark is my therapy. Shouldn't it be for all womankind?

Mum said this will all change when baby Kali arrives. She said that there will be no more shopping for oneself or having the time to do so. I think she's trying to shit me up when she says, "your life is about to go though one major overhaul" and "having a baby is going to hit you like a ton of bricks" - but thankfully I don't scare that easily. Of course, I can't comment much seeing as though it's my first foray into all things baby, but yes, I'm sure some things will go through a bit of a metamorphosis. I mean they're bound to. But one thing that won't is my love for partying.

Just 'cos I will be a Mum doesn't mean that I have to become all good and 'normal' now does it? Maybe for the first month or so while I find my sea legs, but after that, watch out world, Lei Lawson's comin' at ya!
Don't get me wrong, I do realise that I will have to kerb the all-nighters, but if I train Bariş up and give myself a curfew of say 2am, that is more than enough time to get my drink on.

Yes, I think all will be well in Motherhood.

The second thing to cheer me up was a meet up with an old friend from school.
Actually, we were boyfriend/girlfriend when we were just 12 years old. Then again at 18, and again at 23. The last time I saw Jamie was 3 years ago when I was over for my usually summer break and we partied in Chester. We had a great night, but I was reminded why it never worked. He is your typical fella; likes to drink with his mates while the 'little woman' is at home taking care of woman stuff. Well, we all know that that's not how this 'little woman' rolls hence 3rd time (un)lucky. But he will always be a good friend of mine, one of my longest known in fact.

Anyway, we met up at our local and chatted for what seemed like 30 mins but was in fact 4 hours.
It was one of those rare warm days you get during the British summer, so we sat outside in the beer garden lapping it up. During this time, I sunk a shandy.
Seriously, is that so wrong?
I didn't think so, but the looks I caught from others were telling me otherwise. FML, it's not like I go out and drink shandy daily, it's maybe once every second or third week when I allow myself the guilty pleasure, and even then, its only 1, so I couldn't make head nor tail of all the filthy looks flying around.
I suppose that's what happens when one has a pregnant belly and you have a pint glass in front of you – you get judged by the Jeremy Kyle fan club when I'm sure most have done much worse.
Judgey little bitches...

Thankfully, nothing could ruin my high spirits, and after being down in the depths of hormone hell, I was finally a shiny happy person again, shandy in hand!

Random thought: I wonder if I actually have pregnancy hormones, or, I'm simply bi-polar...?

Anyway, the third thing I did to bring myself back into the land of the living was visiting Hannah on Thursday night. We indulged in copious amount of garlic bread, pizza and cups of tea.
How very British of us!
It wasn't the same as one of our usual nights as that would involve vodka instead of tea, and me doing the walk of shame the following morning with mascara down my face.
And I mean the walk of shame from Hannah's house not some random dudes.
Although, in my day...
This time around we were very mature about the way we carried out our evening, well, as mature as two mischievous wannabe youngsters can be when we still believe we're 15 years old. And baby Liv kicked up a storm too, you know, just to say hi Hannah!

Mind you, I'm not ashamed to admit that I may have had somewhat of a freak out again due to all the kicking, because hello, there's a God damn human growing inside me...!

So, freak outs and all, not a bad week truth be told.
Much better than the last and at least I'm out of the blistering heat. No idea when I'm going home yet as I'm waiting for my new passport to arrive. I'll book a flight when it finally gets here. All I can say is it needs to be soon as a lot of airlines don't let you travel after 28 weeks!
Didn't think that through very well before planning my holiday this time around did I?
Another baby brain blunder...

But wouldn't that be something, to give birth on a flight? I heard that if that happened the baby would be given an international passport, never needing a visa to go anywhere - a child of the world as such.
That's pretty cool don't you think?

Anyway, I best get my lard arse up off this sofa as I have an Indian buffet to get ready to gorge upon. Yup, our Sunday afternoon will be spent stuffing our faces at the local Indian with my olds and their mates.

Gotta love friends of the 'rents, they always give such good baby prezzies.

AUGUST

Sunday 6th, 2017
3rd Trimester, Week 28
Current Location: Joe & Wendy's House, Hollywell (North Wales)
Time: 16.51pm

Dear Human dustbin,

As you can see I'm still here, in Blighty that is. I'm currently sat in my parent's friend's house in their office room after being stuffed full of Sunday lunch while listening the rain beat down outside.
And yes, I have taken my lap top with me because this is not my first rodeo.
I made the mistake of not bringing it once before and I will never make that mistake ever again...
Yes, I am aware that I may appear unsociable, but who wants to sit and listen to old people chat all afternoon?
Mind you, Joe and Wendy do look after me terribly well and have bought some lovely stuff for baby Evie, but still, I would find it horrifically boring to be subjected to '*adult*' chat for the rest of the day...

Anyway, as my passport arrived on Monday of last week, I got straight on the flight search and booked my ticket home for this coming Tuesday.

With T minus 2 days to go, this morning I started the huge job of packing. I had to book on a second case as I have been given that much stuff for baby Aurora that 1 case simply wouldn't cut it - 2 may not either!

I've got a steriliser and bottles, a Tommee Tippee perfect prep machine, a changing mat, cot sheets and a 3-piece baby duvet set, baby sleeping bags plus most of Next's baby clothes! As you know I'm a Primark girl, but Mums friends are not. Lucky me, right!
Not to mention the 3 in 1 travel system of which I am taking the car seat home. I can't manage the rest of the pram as I simply don't have the room, so I'm leaving that for the rents to bring in October.

So yes, I have a shit tonne of stuff, and it feels like Christmas, except none of it's mine, well, a few odd pieces of new clothing - but that's it!

One little face that I literally can't wait to see is baby Guch's. Bugger me I've missed him terribly. Barış, on the other hand I'm not so sure of. We had an argument on Thursday night and haven't spoken since.
Looking back now, I see that it was my fault entirely; I couldn't help myself and saw red for the silliest of reasons, but I'll be dammed if I'm letting him know that I know it's my fault.

I tried to play nice yesterday by sending him a Facebook message, but couldn't muster up much niceness, and in return got the same attitude back. Fucker.
Sods law that I need him to put credit on my phone, otherwise I wouldn't bother messaging again.

So, what have we fallen out about?
Restaurant jobs would you believe it!

We were having a hypothetical chat about if we did move to the UK what sort of jobs we would have. Blogging is not going to pay the bills in this country, so I would need a 'real' job (as Dad calls it). So I mentioned to Bariş that we could get bar or restaurant jobs, to which he flat out refused because he reckons he's done his time in the trade.

As everyone that comes into contact with me knows, at this present moment it doesn't take much to set me off, and flat out refusing was like a red rag to a bull.
I informed him that if he refused to work in what may be the only jobs available to us at the time that he would be on the next flight back to Turk land.
I'm cringing now 'cos that is simply a horrific thing to say, but you know me - and, I didn't stop there. I went on to tell him that I am no fuckers cash cow nor am I a visa to the good life. Lei frikkin' Lawson is not your 1 stop shop. So there!

So yes, so I may have flown off the hypothetical handle. Again.
But can I just point out that it's his baby living inside me making me the arsehole that I find myself daily, so really, I'm not to blame.

Note to self: Once baby Blu is born, give yourself a slap so hard that it knocks some decency into you, because you my friend, are a cunt.

Unfortunately, I seem to find myself carrying these bad vibes around with me longer than I ever have before, so the red mist has not quite cleared enough for me to attempt to sort it out just yet. Today it's simply not going to happen.
I know it has to happen, and I know that I need to be the one to make it happen, but, that's not todays problem.
#Nastypregnantbitchstrikesagain

But it hasn't all been doom and gloom, oh hells no - I've been up to quite a bit more than last week seeing as Mum is getting on very well with one crutch now.
Put it this way, the diet starts when I get home as all I've done is eat out, starting on Monday when Hannah took me to the 'Pet Cemetery' for afternoon tea. An odd place to find a Tea room because it wasn't just a clever name, but bugger me it was quite possibly the best afternoon tea I've ever had! I actually felt sick when we left due to

stuffing 4 different cakes down my gullet, as well as the scones and sandwiches!
Greedy bitch.
And, it doesn't stop there...

On Wednesday we hauled arse to our local farm come eatery. I lost my head again when I ordered a starter, main course and a bloody dessert. I don't even know why I did it other than I am a glutinous pig.

Then on Thursday I met up with Camilla the oldest Minger in the world over in Chester. It wasn't a liquid lunch like last year when here, this time around we had a somewhat sensible dining experience in my favourite Italian joint 'Sergios'. Such a quaint little place with real Italian food and real Italian waiters - and once again I stuffed my plate face for sheer greed and certainly not hunger.

It's all fun and games 'till one starts to resemble a weeble – which has totally happened btw.
Maybe eating for 2 really is a thing after all?

I remember a conversation I had with Sister years back about what I would look like as a pregnant fairy. He predicted things well when he said I would balloon up like a blow fish, all chubby cheeks and big boobs.
That fucker was always good with his predictions. It's a shame he can't see me now to rip the piss.

But we did have a good day, Camilla and I, catching up on all things Içmeler.

The greed still doesn't stop there...
It should, but it doesn't.

On Friday night Hannah and I went out for her birthday which we somehow manage to do every year. We decided to eat at home and just do drinks, but when we got to the pub, ole lard arse here was hungry, so we ordered nachos. Then garlic bread, and then another sharer of nachos. Fuck sake, as if we even needed the huge portion of cheesy chips on the walk home!

T'was an odd night as far as nights go.

When you're sober as a judge and you're around a ton of pissed up wankers, it makes for a testing evening. All I wanted to do was join in with the state of inebriation, alas baby Savvy put paid to that.
I did have a Guinness because apparently pregnant women are OK to drink that, but I caught a couple of glances even then.
Once again, I find myself saying judgey little bitches...

And if there was ever a night I needed booze to get through it, this was the night!

I saw things from a different perspective let me tell you. The dudes were loud and leery, either bald or with great big beer bellies, dressed in your typical British style of untucked shirt, jeans and trainers, while swilling back their pints thinking they were the bollocks.
They most certainly were not.
They possibly had great big swollen ones, but that's as far as it goes.

One dirty pig even gobbed on the floor right next to where we were sitting in the beer garden.

Either things have changed drastically since I worked in the very same pub during the winter of '03, or my memories are not quite as accurate as they should be.
I remember that every time we were out in said pub we had a ball, laughing and carrying on with ourselves, and certainly not gobbing. The blokes were decent looking creatures, dressed more sportily, with hair and torte stomachs.
What the fuck happened?

Time happened, that's what!

These are the exact same blokes from back in the day, but age (or marriage) has taken its grim hold. They have let themselves get 'comfortable', and that 'Dear Diary' is not such a pleasant sight to behold.

Thought: I wonder if the same would happen to Barış once ensconced in British life…?

Anyhow, the guy gobbing in front of the whole damn beer garden has nothing to do with comfort and more to do with being a wank stain of society...
I mean, why? Why would you do that?
Dirty fucking bastard.

Anyway, life goes on, and this now brings us up to date with today – Sunday, round at Joe and Wendy's where once again I feel like a human dustbin.

All this eating has got to come to an end otherwise how will I ever rid myself of this holiday weight / baby chub? You hear so many stories about women who have not been able to lose the weight that it puts the fear of God up me - but clearly not enough to stop me from pigging out. Go figure.

Ahh well, home again soon, and because it's so hot I become too damn lazy to cook.

Talking about going home, I decided to shave my v-jayjay today in preparation of the attack of the Husbando the minute I step foot inside the house. On speaking terms or not, I know him well enough by now to know he will have the horn.

But what a fucking job I made of the shave!

What's happened is that my stomach has doubled in size and I couldn't see my fury fairy through the tummy and had to shave the fucker blind!

When I got out of the shower and looked in the mirror, I nearly died of shock! I was greeted with the Texas Chainsaw Massacre - random bits of pubes and blood spurting from all over!
Jesus what a shit show!

This may signify the end of shaving ones punani until one has given birth. Unless Baris wants to take a stab at it, but I'm not so sure I can trust him not to cut my clit off the sly fucker...

Anyway, I can hear my olds preparing to leave so I better pack this shit up. Diarying has certainly speeded up what would usually be a boring afternoon.

So, for today I will bid you adieu.

In my next entry I will be in a warmer climate and with quite possibly a happier soul what with having my furry little piss monster back by my side, and I don't mean my flange here either...

G' Night world and good luck to us all.

P.S. I have had this weird low-pitched hum in my right ear for a few days now. I thought it might be pregnancy related, but upon Sister Googleing it, it seems that it is less pregnancy and more spiritual. Apparently, I am on a journey of awakening and happen to be tuning into the frequencies of the universe.

How fucking exciting!

Sunday, 13th August 2017
Week 29
Current Location: Villa De Guch Pig, Armutalan, Marmaris
Time: 14.14pm

Dear Girl with body complex issues,

Here I am once again, back home where I belong, in the extreme heat with my fur baby and Husbando. Apart from the heat, it sure is good to be home.

I struck lucky on the flight. The check-in guy asked if I was expecting, and luckily for him I am because that could have been totes awks eh...?
Anyway, the nice ole soul upgraded me to an extra legroom aisle seat on row 2 of the aircraft, going on to tell me that his wife has always insisted upon an aisle seat when pregnant due to the constant toilet visits, and how he hopes I have a comfortable flight. Well thank you check-in man, I did have a comfortable flight, and every time I got up to go to the toilet it was like the parting of the red sea with every person in front pushing me forwards in line.
I never had to queue for the loo once!
Although I am obviously expecting, I wasn't expecting such good nature from everyone around.

Mental Note: I must remember to pay it forwards for other females in the pudding club.

I arrived home to a Husbando that pretended to have cleaned the house with the insatiable urge to get me directly in the sack. And after all that travelling you would think the fucker would leave me alone 'till at least the following day, or, I'd had a shower!
Alas, I knew what I was in for when I Facebook checked in at Dalaman airport and he was straight on the blower asking how long it would be till I got home, a little too overenthusiastically for someone who had been giving me the silent treatment for 5 days prior...

So, since arriving back I've had the washing machine on 3 times as Husbando failed to listen to washing instructions and refused to wash a single thing for 3 whole weeks, I've scrubbed the house within an inch of its life because it was pretty bloody rank even with the 'fake cleaning', I've walked the hind legs off Gucci as I could see in his eyes that Bariş hadn't taken him on the long walks that was claimed, and finally, I've performed my wifely duties twice!
And in this heat, that's quite an accomplishment!

Wednesday nearly killed me though...
It started out well because while at our scheduled Gynae appointment luck was on our side when we finally saw sproggies face for the very first time!
Thank the good Lord above that she doesn't seem to have any facial defects. Her nose looks cute as a button, and more to the point not oversized (thank you Jesus!). She has a delightful diamond shape to her face with chubby little cheeks that I just want to pinch, and the most delightful rosebud lips you have ever seen.
Colour me très blessed!

Oh the wonders of modern technology letting us see all of this, but fuck me, what have I become? Excitement seems to have taken a hold and I now resemble a clucking fucking duck! And that 'Dear Diary' is an alien feeling to a wannabe socialite such as myself...

The doc was happy with the progress although he mentioned that baby Lennox was a tad on the large size, advising me to come back the following day to check my blood sugar.
Oh God, not that old chestnut.

The last time I was tested was before I went away, failing miserably on the first glucose test, apparently showing sky high signs that I had pregnancy diabetes. I wasn't surprised considering the amount of chocolate, crisps and general junk food that had laced my pregnant body.
So, the dietician in the 'Ahu Hetman' hospital put me on a strict diet for a week before testing me once more.

I can honestly say that was the worst week of my life.

I was hungry literally all the time, I had no energy, I was snappy and pretty much suffering from eater's remorse. Both Barış and I were particularly glad when that week was over and I could resume normal eating habits of pizza, cake and donuts again, and nasty Lei was put back in her box.
Jesus I was a vicious little sod.

Although the test after the diet had me well under the radar, they told me to continue with the stupid diet anyway, which I said I would but immediately knew that I wouldn't because it was a pile of pish.

So, I ate to my heart's content in the UK and now baby Melodi is a big bugger.
Fuck my life, it could only happen to me...

After the hospital visit we did the usual and hit up 'Yunus' for lunch where we went on to further discuss moving to the UK, but this time with no mention of working in bars or restaurants. I mean it's a bit too soon to be rocking the boat don't you think?

My calmer approach worked and we had a civil conversation about it. I told Barış about an offer from my olds, that if we do decide to move back, we can move into their flat in town for free.

Bugger bloody me. It's starting to feel as if I'm moving to the UK.
How did this happen?
How can this be?
Shit the bed dude.
Shit that bloody bed.

Barış went on to state in no uncertain terms that even if he couldn't get a visa, he still wants me, Guch and baby Josey to go without him as he is super concerned about the state of Turkey and what's going to happen next. As if I would leave my ole ball and chain here on his own, but I get his train of thought.

And before you start to wonder, no, Bariş is not trying to get me gone so he can get another woman in (I hope). That's just not the way he is built (please God).

From 'Yunus' we went to the bank and then on to food shop in 'Kipa', as low and behold there was fuck all in the fridge other than water.
Why are men so shit when it comes to looking after themselves?

Whilst in 'Kipa' my legs turned to jelly and I just knew I had to get home before I decided to sit on the floor in the middle of the cake aisle for all eternity...
Now I'm not blaming pregnancy for this lack of energy, after all, extreme heat is draining, but I'm sure baby Lyra is not exactly helping...

And when I did finally get home, I did sweet F.A. for what was left of the day. I couldn't even be bothered to cook, so for dinner we feasted on melon and 'Helva' because Bariş couldn't put anything else together in the kitchen.
He tries the little dear.

On Thursday I went back for the next blood sugar test, and, to my utter surprise I was within the range of normal! Colour me the happiest gal on the planet, especially after my UK pig out! Screw you diet, screw you!

FYI: If I have learnt anything about hospital visits while pregnant, is that here, they are super anal about food and pretty much everything else. I suppose it's not a bad thing to be concerned about literally everything, but seriously, when will he tell us to stop having sex?

I've just had a thought, what if that day never comes and at 9 months pregnant Bariş is still sticking it to me?
Fuck that shit man, I've had enough sex now to last a lifetime, well, at least till I'm no longer pregnant and it's winter again!

I wonder if it would have been different if we had seen the female Gynae?
I bet she would have taken pity on poor ole spunk bucket Lei... What a shame I can't change doctors, but with so little time to go I suppose I will just have to put up and shut up. Or fake a few more backaches and stomach pains – that always does the trick.

Anyway, my Gynae mentioned that if the baby weighs over 4 kilos when I'm due to give birth that it would have to be by caesarean. I always wanted a caesarean for as long as I can remember as I could get a tummy tuck at the same time, however after finding out that the recovery period is 6 weeks or so, I'm hoping above all hope that baby Amelie is under that weight and I am able to go au naturale and push my baby shaped water melon out of my shrivelled up ole minge. With ridiculously strong drugs of course.

Well done to the strong women of this world that do it without, but this pain feared female requires drugs, and plenty of them. In fact, just keep them pumping through my veins until *I* say I'm ready to go cold turkey.

And then came Friday which saw me having to cancel my Turkish lesson and hair appointment, as can you believe it, I may have got my first dose of morning sickness – at 29 weeks bloody pregnant and all! I definitely missed it in the first trimester, but please universe, don't see fit to give it to me now. I promise not to subject Husbando to too much shit, just please don't punish me in my last couple of months...

Oh, and Turkish lesson?
Yup that's right. I decided on the day I found out I was preggers that I need to get this Turkish polished.
I honest to God didn't think it was going to be as hard as it is. I thought with all I have under my belt that I would be there 2 months and then be fluent. Shock horror – I'm not, and nowhere near it. Me thinks me may have bitten off more than me can chew, especially with my baby brain getting worse daily. But I won't give up, I've ploughed too much cash into it now to simply quit. And a

quitter Lei Lawson is not – a cunt quite possibly yes, but a quitter - never!

Thankfully, I managed to keep my breakfast down on Saturday. Thinking of it now, it was mostly yogurt that I spewed, so maybe the yogurt was off and it wasn't morning sickness after all? Who the hell knows, but I just thank my lucky stars that I didn't have to cancel my day out with Kate because that would have been just turds.

We jumped in Kastro my car and headed over to 'Asparan' for a day of feeding our faces and swimming.
'Asparan' is like a little oasis in the summer. It's out in nature, surrounded by pretty much nothing, has a park and animals to keep the kids entertained and a great big massive pool with slides. All this only a 20-minute drive out of Marmaris!
It's kind of a hidden gem because you don't see many tourists there at all, and if you go on a weekday, it's pretty much empty!

And yes, ole fat heffer here got the belly out in public and hit the pool.

By Christ I don't think I have ever been as self-conscious as I was yesterday. Seriously, I hate getting the belly out, even when I'm not pregnant, so you can just imagine how I felt now that I resemble ten-ton Tessie!

Kate said I looked beautiful and had a 'blooming' pregnancy glow about me.
That Kate is bloody liar 'cos I know exactly how I looked in that ugly bikini with my belly the size of a bishop with its protruding green veins, and not forgetting the dirty dark line running straight though the middle...

Don't get me wrong, I'm not slating all pregnant women in bikinis, oh hells no, just this one. I have seen many an attractive bump poolside previously, and of course in my mind's eye, I thought I would look just as lovely.
Nope – wrong on that score.

All I see when I look in the mirror is a great big bulky lass that looks like she ate all the pies. An attractive pregnant woman I am not. Plus, I really did eat all the pies because I can't bloody help myself.

But we did have a lovely chilled out day, lies and all, ending it in Starbucks with a 'Strawberries and Cream' frappuccino each. Thankfully no members of the rival gang were in situ. It would have been just my luck for them to see me looking like a dishevelled skip rat dressed in shit 'cos none of my clothes fit, trying not to waddle when I walk.
#SmallMercies.

Anyway, I've a question that's been bothering me – why do pregnant women get so sodding tired all the time?
I got home at 7pm yesterday and had to have a 2-hour nap on the sofa immediately. I'm finding that this has become a daily occurrence, and even when I've not been out, I'm buggered. I'm not even over-exerting myself - the heat puts paid to that, yet still I find myself breathless with a racing heart.
And I've noticed that come 10.30pm I am ready for bed and find it almost impossible to put one foot in front of the other to get there.

Yup, my days of night time activities are on pause for the time being. I can't stand in the bathroom to put my day time make-up on, let alone maintain an erect position for the two-hour night time face lift!

I guess exhaustion is simply part and parcel of being up the duff. But all of this is OK because I don't have much longer to go; thankfully this is not a forever situation. For now, I can totally embrace day time activities because I have to. It's not like I'm locking myself indoors missing out on anything other than partying, which let's face it, will still be there when I am me and only me again.

And finally, after all of the above waffle, we come to today, Sunday. Although I've not fallen out with Barış I think he may have seen his arse because this morning while in bed, he was coming in for a cuddle and I near ripped his head off. The sweat was pouring out of me and having him lump his arms, legs and body around me was nearly enough to bring back the dose of sickness from Friday. Poor bastard didn't know what hit him when blind rage flew out of my gob before I could even think about it.

That. Poor. Man.

I think he (as well as me) will be glad when the day comes that baby Summer enters this world and my overheating body and fiery hormones go back to normal. This shit could not continue long-term because if it did, it would end in divorce or death.
I'm betting death.
The only one in this house that doesn't get the wrath of Lei is Guch. He is simply too delightful to hate on, even though he pissed on every corner of my cream shaggy rug in the sitting room whilst I was away. Fuck knows how long it's been there but it's safe to say that whether Barış knew about it or not, he simply did not get the bleach out to clean it up.
Fucking men.

And there I go again!

And with that I think it's time to retire to the sofa. Now that I don't have Love Island to watch I've started on Big Brother. I have never in my life watched Big Brother, but do you know what, I'm really getting into it.

So, ciao for now mi amigo, next time I'm hoping there will be less agg to report of.

Saturday, 19th August 2017
Week 30
Time: 15.43

Dear Sleepless in the Marm farm,

I've just been having a catch-up with me ole mucker Jenny via Facebook messenger. You remember Jen don't you? She ended up leaving Turkey back in October in the hopes that she could get over her ex.
She hasn't. Got over him that is.
Since leaving she has not been out on 1 single date. She has been asked of course, the girl is a looker, alas each and every one she turns down. I swear she lives in hope that the ex is going to make some grand gesture. He's not though.
He's a cunt but treats her like she's the cunt, yet she can't get him out of her head.
I swear the whole 'treat 'em mean, keep 'em keen' works a charm, and not just on our Jen. I mean look at me circa 2011 and there you have it!

Anyway, that girl always puts me in a good mood. Not that I was in a bad mood, just a Saturday mood, which was sick of cleaning while drenched in piss sweat with baby Khloe beating me up from the inside.

Jen is hopefully coming over mid-September for a couple of weeks. I say hopefully as this won't be her first attempt of the year to come - oh no, in June she got all the way to Dalaman airport to be promptly kicked back out again.
Remember she had that residency issue where she didn't renew it and was 3 months over?
Yup – that came back to bite her on the arse.
She found out on arrival at Dalaman that she had been given a ban from Turkey and the only way to sort the issue out was to go to the Turkish consulate in London.

The hotel, flights, new holiday wardrobe, the lot were totally wasted, and Jenny was absolutely devastated. If only they had told her when she left so she could have sorted this issue out beforehand!
She knew she would have a fine to pay, but being banned? WTF!

In all honesty, I think she was more upset at being deported what with the humiliation of being escorted onto the next available aircraft by the police. That can't have been fun.
And then having to endure the 4.5-hour flight in floods of tears with nosey onlookers wondering just what she had *'done'* - just awful!

I woke up the following morning super excited to be seeing my friend later that day, but upon checking Facebook I saw it wasn't to be.
As much as Jen was gutted, so was I.
We had a lengthy video chat when she found herself back at Birmingham airport, and vowed that it wasn't the last that Turkey had seen of her this year.

So, since then she has jumped through hoops trying to rectify the problem and has hauled ass to London to hand over the mountain of paperwork required.

Current status: Limbo.
Fucking red tape…!

I'm positive though that once a decision has been made that she will be here like shit off a shovel. That girl loves Turkey (and her ex) too much to be told NO this season. Put it this way, I'm keeping my fingers, toes and womb crossed that all goes well. After all, I'm just dying for her to meet the bump in person!

Anyway, life goes on, and so has this week.
It's been hot, sticky and I can't wait for October to arrive. I'm hoping I will be able to sleep better then as now I'm finding it virtually impossible for two reasons: heat and pregnancy.

The heat speaks for itself – August is a shit month, but the pregnancy stuff I'm quite baffled with. I simply can't get comfortable. I'm tossing and turning all night long with 23 trips to the pisser in-between.
This does not make for a well-rested sloth come morning.
Thankfully Bariş is up and out to work most mornings before my feet touch the ground, and he's come to learn pretty fucking quickly that if he's home then he better have cleared up his shit before I wake.
It's not like I'm being a cunt without reason, I mean who wants to be waking up to someone else's late-night snacking destruction?

So, in an aid to get me some kip I'm currently trying the Sister Google recommended 'pillow between the legs' trick come bed time. Not sure what it does exactly but it's quite comfortable, so that's how I shall continue.
But it doesn't really help that I have a newly sheered Guch who feels less like a Yeti and more like a happy naked person, because all he wants to do is snuggle all night.
Not into Bariş, only into me.

I would kick him off the bed but when I see his little face flooded with cuteness, resting his head on the pillow right next to mine, it's virtually impossible to kick him off because he is simply too adorable. And because I just love that face, I choose the sleepless nights since as long as my little fur baby is happy, then so am I.

But I'm not happy am I 'cos I can't friggin' sleep!
Catch 22 strikes again.

Maybe Bariş should volunteer to sleep in the spare room and leave me and baby Guch with more space? After all, I have been booted out of bed so rudely by the pair of them before now...

And by the time October comes, although the heat won't keep me awake, I will be in the last month of pregnancy, and I have been informed that sleep probably will not wish to visit much then either.
Oh, lucky me.

So, what's a slovenly couch potato to do FFS?!

Ahh fuck it, it's all part and parcel of 'training' for when baby Tailor arrives.
But you never know, I may have a baby that is as sloth-like as I. Wouldn't that be a pip?

So, due to the stinking humidity I have not wanted to venture far this week, especially during day time hours, so indoors I stayed on Monday and Tuesday.

Tuesday was a particularly productive day as I emptied out my side board cabinet in the nursery ready to fill with all things baby. What a gross job that turned out to be and I gave myself stitch whilst doing so.
Who would have thought you could get stitch from a light bit of boxing up? Certainly not me, so I consulted Sister G because it was bound to be baby Lia related.
Yup – ligament pain apparently.
But it did get me out of cooking and taking Guch out for walks. Ole Husbando stepped up and was golden, taking over my side of the work when he got home from his.

He's a good egg you know, especially when trying to cheer me up by showing me his 'willy-copter'. I felt too bad to tell him that the laughter made my stitch worse...

Wednesday we didn't have the luxury of staying indoors as we had stuff to do and it was Barış's only day off to do it.
Firstly, let me point out that when I got out of the shower and inspected my ever-growing body in the mirror, I noticed that once again the nips have jumped in size. As if those fuckers weren't big enough already!
One day soon I'm going to wake up and they will have taken over the entire top half of my body and I will be using them as eyes. Honest to God, they have literally covered most of my breasticles now.

Barış near shit himself when he walked into the bathroom to find me slavering bio oil on my great big belly, and then when one of my new

nip eyes winked at him it was enough to send him running for cover, ensuring that he will never want to see what's underneath my clothing ever again.
Bonus!
Poor bugger sat stroking Guch to calm himself down and I'm sure I heard him mutter something about being married to an alien...

After that experience we went about our business as usual. Well I did, but Barış didn't actually recover until last night.
Anyway, we managed to get our chores done and stopped off at 'Meryem Anna' in Marmaris centre for a bite to eat. What's good about 'Meryem' is that they have all home cooked food, so being the lazy hash slinger that I am these hot pregnant days, I thought let's eat our dinner at lunch time and then I wouldn't have to be tied to the kitchen in the evening.

A quote from Bill Gates seems pretty fitting here: "I choose a lazy person to do a hard job because a lazy person will find an easy way to do it".
Never a truer word spoken when it comes to me and cooking these days Bill...

And after filling our bellies we hit 'Tespo' cash 'n' carry because I heard they were the cheapest place to stock up on nappies, wipes and baby milk.

Whilst in the UK Hannah gave me a tip to start bulk buying that sort of stuff now so it wouldn't be too much of a hit on the old shopping bill later. Although it was a great idea, I nearly had a heart attack at just how costly these baby bits were.

There are no child tax credits (or whatever they are known by these days) in this country, well you can't call 20tl a month child benefit, so I won't! We are doing this all on our own, so it comes as a bit of a shock to find that what I originally budgeted for nappies, etc, came to only about half of the reality.

Fuck me, baby shit is expensive!

If I was breastfeeding I suppose it would work out cheaper, but I'm not so I will just have to suck it up (excuse the pun).

Why am I not breastfeeding?
Because eww gross and absolutely not.

Of course I know what society has told me about Mothers milk being the best, but loads of my buddies didn't breast feed and their kids have turned out A-OK.
I'm not regarding it as a massive deal, that however, can't be said for the Turks around me, but, that's none of my business…

People keep saying that I will change my mind once baby Jasmine pops out, and that all I will want to do is stick my huge fucking nip in her mouth and let her suckle away.
I say no-sir-ee and now I have cringed myself out and feel slightly sick about it all.

It's a personal choice and one that I'm sticking to - sorry Mum.

Thursday was a sofa day as I must have over-exerted myself on the Wednesday as the stitch was back. So, I did what any normal person would and turned the A/C on whilst binge watching season 17 of Big Brother.
Good times.

Friday was a bit different as I had a busy day lined up. Number one on my list was my first Turkish lesson after 4 weeks off and I'm not afraid to admit that it was a task and a half. My brain is like diarrhoea right now so just how I got through that lesson is beyond me.

From there I called in at Sandie's house where she plied me full of tea and cake while we caught up. Even after 2 hours we still had not finished, but I had to go as I was meeting Kate and Audrey at 6.30pm for bowling and food on the marina.
And what a good night we had.
Who needs men to take you bowling when you have your girls!

We had some laughs, deep conversation, food, and yes, I had myself a shandy because it was fucking hot and I wanted one.
But just the one.

When we're all together, nothing is off the table. Our chat goes from discussing what bollocks the rival gang has been posting on Facebook, through to the most intelligent conversation I think I have ever had about stuff like quantum physics and the universe.
Yup, our conflab is as broad as the day is long, and I can't get enough. But sometimes, like Friday night for example, I noticed that Kate can get a little, well, to put it politely, a bit know-it-all-y.
And oh, how I hate know-it-all's...
Maybe just my prickly pregnancy picking up on things that don't exist, but I shall keep an eye on that because at this age and stage I don't take any prisoners.

And that brings us to today - Saturday.
Kimmy has just informed me that she is on her way to Marmaris and do I want to go for brunch tomorrow. Yes, I most certainly do as I love food, and I've not seen Kimmy since before Blighty when I stayed with her in Fethiye for a few days. I don't get to see her face so often what with her being based all the way down yonder this season, so brunch was by far a fantastic idea.
And apparently, she has bought some outfits for baby Kady and is just dying to show them to me. Yipeeeee!

Seriously that's one hell of a pregnancy perk you know, people buying all sorts of baby related artefacts for you.
Who knew?!

And my mad Saturday night plans?
Well actually tonight just happens to be double date night with Julia and Zafer down in Hisaronu (but not the Fethiye one). They say it's cooler down there, so we are taking the 20-minute drive out to see them for dinner on the beach.

You see, I can be civilized when I must.

P.S: The weird hum I was experiencing in the UK?
Gone.
I wonder if I have finally spiritually awakened or it just decided to give up on a lost cause?
I don't feel any different, so I'm guessing they've given up.
I am, on the other hand, still seeing all sorts of repetitive numbers, so somethings still afoot...
Prophet baby, here we come.

Saturday 26th August, 2017
Week 31
Weight: 73.8 Kilos
Time: 15.16pm

Dear Birthday girl,

Happy fucking birthday Lei.

I always thought birthdays were supposed to be joyous occasions? Oh how wrong one can be!

Contrary to my Facebook post earlier, I am not exactly enjoying my day. Whether I have me an extra special dose of birthday pregnancy hormones, or it's because I know I can't go out and party – this birthday has turned out to be a total bag of bollocks, and it's not even 3.30pm!

I had better explain...

Firstly, Kimmy isn't here as it's not as if she can drive up from Fethiye every weekend, secondly Barış is on lates so he can't take me out for dinner, thirdly Sister is not around to indulge in my birthday doom because, well, he's dead, and fourthly Lacie is loving life across the ocean having her very own birthday every day.
Yup, today I'm feeling like a pile of dog shite that someone has skidded through and smeared across the pavement.

So yeah, happy fucking birthday Lei...

I make it sound as if it's all bad when it's not; not really.
Barış and I went for birthday brunch earlier to 'Şahin Tepe' on the mountain. It would have been lovely had he not been filled with attitude, which had a knock-on effect on my frame of mind.

Yup, it was clear that neither of us truly wanted to be there, so we sat in pretty much silence for the duration. He tried to make small talk, but it just wasn't happening.

Maybe if he had wished me happy birthday when he got up things would have started off better?
Alas, I'm still waiting now.
I suppose I should be used to it as he never goes in for birthdays, but still, pretending to care that I have turned a year wouldn't have gone a miss. Especially a pregnant year.
Cunt.

Of course I took the obligatory photos and uploaded them to Facebook so it didn't look like I did fuck all for my birthday, but really I wish that I had of done fuck all as by all accounts brunch was pretty shit.

So, I suppose it is all bad after all…

I told my buds earlier in the week that I wasn't planning a dinner or anything, and those closest to me know that I can barely make it past 10.00pm before an attack of the yawns, so I don't see the point in going out for a celebratory meal when the pictures would show less of a celebration and more of a crap doo that no one wants to be part of. And let's face it; a birthday dinner without booze would be a crap doo that no one wants to be part of…!

I will have to pretend that this year didn't happen and that next year is actually my 37th. Not a bad idea, skipping a year. I wonder if the wrinkles can be convinced to do the same?

Anyway, enough doom and gloom – let's attempt to change this mood of mine with some positive thoughts.

Attempt #1: Gucci.
If anyone can alter my mood, Gucci can. Man alive he is a cute little ball of energy that I don't know how I would get through life without. But one day I'll have to as he's going to die and leave me alone to deal with Barış and baby Sutton and I really don't know what I'm going to do then.

Oh FFS Lei – you were supposed to be turning your mood around not sitting here blubbering at the thought of losing Guch.
That's right; I have great big tears rolling down my fat fucking face right at this very instant.
WTF is going on with me?
How can it be that right here, right now I'm a complete sobbing frikkin' mess? And can I point out that my sobs are great big shoulder heaving things that I can barely type through, not just small snotty little snivels.
Fuck sake.

It doesn't help that I've just looked in the mirror and now resemble Alice Cooper what with the big black eyes and mascara streaming down my face. Also, one eyebrow has rubbed off. Not the entire eyebrow of course, just the brow shadow, but a cunt I do look…

Sometimes, being pregnant is not the *glowing* period it's made out to be.
Well, today it's not at least.

Attempt #1 status: Epic fail.

Attempt #2:   Baby Alexis has just booted me extremely hard – quite possibly for being a moaning ole munter, and quite right too.
It's actually made me feel slightly better knowing that I need to pull myself outta this shit, not just for me, but for her too. I mean who wants a drivelling mess of a Mum slobbing around the house feeling sorry for herself?
I wonder if she knows I'm having a birthday crisis and it's affecting her mood as well?
At least being kicked quite literally in the cunt has stopped the sobs.

Can I just mention though that my punani is like a fucking slip 'n' slide these days? What the fuck is with all the extra discharge man? I'm having to change my 'Bridget Joneses' twice a day due to the extra filth falling out because I will not invest in panty liners. Fuck me, they are something my Mum would wear, not me, not this newly turned 37-year-old pregnant wannabe socialite!

Barış off course thinks it's great as we no longer need lube for sex, me on the other hand, I think it's quite disgusting, and although I absolutely hate it, I would prefer the 'gob on yer fanny' technique to this...

Attempt #2 status: Success.

Mental note: Talking about the state of one's minge really can pull the most depressed of pregnant twat's right again.
But pregnant twat doesn't make sense does it? A twat is a pregnant fish isn't it? So I'm calling myself a pregnant pregnant fish?
Oh my days, just turn on Big Brother and be done with the day…

19.32pm
Right then – seeing as the crying has come to a halt and I've had a word with myself, let me tell you about my week so far:

Saturday night was a hot and sticky mess of a night where Husbando and I thought we would get some cool in the windy village of Hisaronu, but of course the wind decided not to visit that night. Talk about sweating one's tits off…
But a lovely evening with Julia and Zafer was had none the less. We had a delightful dinner on the beach and then went back to their house for coffee.
It was civilised, mature and rather adult of us.

Lately I feel like screaming 'will the real Lei Lawson please stand up!' because, I fear, that Barış and I are morphing into my parents what with all this maturity.
What the fuck has become of us?
I need to sort myself out once Baby Sun cream has arrived. This ridiculousness simply cannot continue…

On Sunday Kimmy and I went for brunch at 'Çinar', an old favourite brunch spot of ours that is a 20-minute drive out of Marmaris towards the airport. Nestled on a quiet village road, it was cool, shaded and windy, just the way a nearly 8-month pregnant fairy requires it.

After that we hit up 'Starbucks' for a Frappuccino and then a walk around the marina.
This did not end well.
By the time our mooch had come to a close I'd convinced myself that I had preeclampsia. My ankles had turned into cankles and I had sausage fingers! Yup, I had turned into a human hot air balloon, all puffed up and sweaty.
Kimmy wanted to run me to the hospital there and then, but I said no, let's wait to see how it all looks after sitting with my feet up in the air conditioning for a few hours.
Thankfully, the swelling came down some, but fuck me seeing my hands and feet in that state was a shock to the system!

I think it's safe to say that this pregnancy has most definitely started to affect me...

So, because of ole cankles, Monday I had a day indoors, but Tuesday saw me back round at Sandie's as we still had more to catch up on.

I really do think the world of Sandie, she is just so chilled out and laid back about life. She reminds me a bit of Sister and I am super glad I have her around seeing as Sister is not.

Wednesday, although it was Husbando's day off, I didn't have the will nor motivation to leave the house. We had stuff to do, but I simply couldn't force myself to do it. Also, I was going out for dinner with Lucy, Kat and Sonia so needed to conserve my energy.

August heat = miserable times.

Thankfully it dropped a couple of degrees for the evening and for the first time since I got back from the UK, I was able to wear my leggings without sweating my fanny off.

As it happens, it turned out to be a somewhat odd evening at 'Yali Beach', where the girls went on to give me their birth stories', or should I say horror stories?
Can I just ask why though? Why try to put the fear of God up me when I am so close to the finishing line? Such a shits trick, but their plan didn't work, and I've remained super calm about the whole damn thing. Quite unlike me that's fo' shizzle. I wonder if it's because I'm still in disbelief that I'm actually going to have myself a real live baby?
But more to the point, why are these girls trying to scare me shitless? Is that what girls do these days?
No wonder I keep myself to myself when this is the sort of shit you have to deal with when dining out with half of a clique.

Did I not mention? Opps, scrambled egg brain strikes again!

So, in fact, Lucy, Kat and Sonia make up half of 'The Golden Group'. Lucy is my neighbour and I have known Kat and Sonia for years, but never the less, a clique they are part of.

Although I was included in most of the evenings conversation, there were times when I wanted to claw my eyeballs out of their sockets and go home because they turned the convo on the other half of the clique - you know, the half that wasn't dining with us.
It was awkward as bloody arse and I don't mind telling you that I told them so. I mean who wants to sit at a table and listen to them rip the shit out of their so-called friends (who I know quite well to by the way), but also for them to tell only half a story so I couldn't even get the full gist?

I don't think they were expecting my outburst, but come on, if you're going to talk crap about your mates, at least give the guest the full bloody deets...

Mind you, I did join in when they laid into the rival gang of Larissa and her muppets, AKA 'The Marmaris Elite'. I enjoyed that portion of the evening immensely, because although I'm not a gal that likes to hear friends talk shit about friends, I am still me, and this 'ere me dislikes the rival gang with a passion hehe!

So, if asked to give my very unwanted opinion on it all, this is how it shall be summed up:
Clique life = A cunts life.
Once again, thanks, but no thanks.

And back to the normal, after having a 'Netflix and Guch' day on Thursday, once I had bumbled my way through my Turkish lesson on Friday, I met up with John for a light lunch in 'Yilmaz' in the centre of town. He's also been in the UK for quite some time, so it was great to catch up.
I'm trying to convince him to sell me his car because as much as I love Kastro, having a 2-door car with a teeny weenie boot is not quite practical for when Baby Jayne arrives. I think I may have worn him down as he said he will pop up next week for a test drive.

So, this brings us up to today – my birthday, for which I am doing nothing apart from still feeling sorry for myself.

In other unrelated news:
#1: I think my boobs are barren because I read on Sister Google that I should have started to leak a milky type substance by now, but there ain't ball all going on in this bosom of mine.
In fact, my boobs don't feel hard or painful as described that they should.
Of course I will take this as a blessing and not a curse as I'm not breastfeeding anyway, but do you think there could be something wrong with my udders?

I've had a couple of jabbing pains in the last couple of weeks, so I thought something may be a foot, but sod all has come from it. I do, however, doubt very much that anything could leak through the nip crust that is ever present recently...

I suppose I could ask the Gynae when I visit on Tuesday and get his take on it all. But then he may want to inspect a tit and I really don't fancy that.

No, I shall consult Sister G about it further instead.

#2: Talking about tits, when scrolling through Facebook yesterday a post on one of the Marmaris groups caught my attention. It was about a trip seller that had messaged a female holiday maker regarding dropping off her excursion tickets, and while he was at it would she show him her tits - and that was just the start of it!

The holiday maker quite rightly screen shotted the message and decided to name and shame the dirty perv by posting said message to the group.
I tell you what, I was shocked to read some of the comments underneath. What the fuck is wrong with people when they defend this arsehole by saying 'how out of character this is' and 'never in my 5 years booking with him has he ever spoken to me like this'.
Calm down Dorris, just because he never sent you a dick pic doesn't mean that he didn't commit this string of smut. It may simply mean that he found you undeserving of seeing his 'monster'. Ever thought about that love?

And, I've got news for you Dorris – this ole love rat is a dirty bastard and always has been.
This nasty assed toe rag that you happen to consider a close personal comrade and visit every year when you're on holiday is not your *'best friend'* as he puts it. You are neither his Sister nor his Aunty. He simply wants to charm the cash out of you whilst charming the knickers off the tourists that do tickle his fancy.

Did you ever stop and wonder why you're called by a nick name Dorris? I bet you thought it was a term of endearment, didn't you? Unfortunately not my dear, it's because he doesn't remember your real name as you're only here for two weeks and are insignificant to his life, unless of course you bring him goodies and duty free that you never charge him for because he is your *friend*.
Mark my words, there are a million other 'J-Lo's, Shakira's, Del Boy's and Cheeky Buggers' out there Dorris. You, dear lady, are not special.
#SorryNotSorry

But more worryingly than the above is the fact that these 'charmers' have become so very lazy and/or complacent.
Whatever happened to the cheese ball chat up lines and offering to take said tourist out for a drink in order to have their wicked way? After all, they won't be out of pocket, 'rich' ole tourist would be paying for the drinks...

And that is where I shall leave it for today 'Dear Diary'. I believe my voice of doom has offended enough for one day.

It's time to move onto the sofa, get the ice cream out of the freezer and add more fat to my ever-increasing body. I mean FFS – I have put on 10 kilos so far this pregnancy.
All I can say is this diet coffee that I've bought better live up to its hype.

#GetaFuckingGripLei

SEPTEMBER

Sunday 3rd, 2017
Week 32
Time: 11.08am

Dear Shamu,

Just look at the time! 11.08am! What the bloody F is happening to me?

I've been up since the butt crack of dawn and done all my TV watching already because:
   a) Husbando is a selfish mo fo as he has six alarms going off before getting up to go to work, all set in 20-minute intervals, keeping me wide awake from the first alarm,
and
   b) Sleep is becoming more elusive by the day as I simply can't get comfortable.

Why am I being punished so?

And to make matters worse, trying to get out of bed is becoming more ridiculous by the day. I'm waking the entire block flapping

around like a polar bear who's fallen flat on his back on the ice.
Jesus, the state of me...
There has got to be an easier way to get out of bed than this. And up from the sofa. And the toilet. Let's just say pretty much everywhere.

It doesn't help that every time I go to the lav Gucci jumps onto the bed and I near kill the little fucker when I get back in... Not from a near squashing episode 'cos he is clued up to that by now; but just like Shamu the whale flopping back into the water - the bed bounces poor ole Guch five foot in the air when my lard arse hits it.
I live in a bloody cartoon FFS.

And Barış?
Oblivious to it all as he is sound asleep, and nothing can wake him - only the sixth and final fucking alarm of the morning.
Arse.

Another thing I have found recently is that the breathlessness is becoming worse.
Yesterday I was in 'Kipa' doing the weekly shop and had to lean on the shopping trolley for fear of collapsing. I had only just walked through the main entrance from being sat on my arse in the car, and prior to that, sat on my arse in the house. In fact, I feel breathless right now and I'm sat on my arse in the kitchen.

And while we are on the subject of pregnancy, I must tell you when I haven't felt baby Tallulah boot me in the womb for a couple of hours, it certainly puts the shitters up me. So I did some research on Sister Google, and apparently, you can wake your baby up by drinking cold ice water. Surely that can't be a nice experience for the poor little sod?
It reminds me of doing the ice bucket challenge and that was a cunt and a half, so can you imagine how poor baby Rayna would feel getting woken up in such a way?
But that's not to say I haven't given it a go.
Oh yes, sometimes I fear the worst and panic takes over, so ice water is drunk by the gallon.

All credit to Sister G, being woken like that is a great way to get the little mo fo wriggling around, proving that she is indeed alive and kicking.

Shit, I'm a bad Mum already…

But bad Mum or not, my skin is simply loving life right now!
As you know I'm prone to a spot or 20 and since being up the spout I've had not 1 spot - not bloody 1! It's fair to say that my skin is glowing, and I swear I'm not taking the piss!
Who knew that this glowing shit could be an actual thing?!

Anyway, enough of that for now, let me fill you in on this week's events:

From my birthday through till Husbando's day off (Wednesday), I did absolutely nothing. As I had been indoors and rested, I forced myself into making a day of it, so, out and about I went with the ole ball and chain.
It was the start of Byram week with Victory day being the first of the holidays, so as you can imagine town was heaving. That didn't stop us from doing our thing and hitting up 'Oh Yes' on the marina for lunch, visiting the loo in 'Burger King' only to find that they have gone and enabled a password lock causing me to near wet myself 15 whole minutes after having a pee in 'Oh Yes', then heading over to 'Dr. Gelato's' for ice-cream (and a pee), and finally over to 'Blue Port' to pick up a nappy bin for the nursery. And I had a pee.

A productive day for my bladder and extremities!

Thursday I decided to stay indoors to rest the cankles because Friday Barış was off again due the second holiday of the week: Kurban Byram. Yup, my least favourite holiday because of all the murdering that takes place right on one's door step.

I have learnt from past mistakes not to stay home on this Byram just in case those neighbours of mine decide to sacrifice a goat on my threshold again; so, off to 'Yunus' for a late brunch we went.

In the restaurant Barış surprised me by informing me that he is on the verge of becoming vegetarian – and that's without any coaxing from me!

I remember that feeling of being on the verge, yet still fancying a Maccy D's cheeseburger but knowing it was wrong. Mind you, I was 12 at the time.
I think I may have slipped 2 or 3 times and indulged in said cheeseburger, but it came to a head when I ordered my last, opened it up and couldn't stomach the smell let alone put it in my mouth.

It's funny how that all came about, vegetarianism I mean.
Mum said I came home from school one day after being shown a video of an abattoir, then declared no more meat for little Lawson! And that was literally it.
She was furious with the school of course, even went to see the head master, but, the damage had been done.

That was quite possibly the one and only thing that I took from school.
Algebra was never used again because why the hell would it be? So having vegetarianism stick with me 25 years later is an accomplishment for this 'ere naughty school kid.
Not that the school showing that video had anything to do with promoting vegetarianism, oh no, it was more about handling meat if my memory serves.
Thinking back now, why on earth would they show such shit to young impressionable kids…?

Anyway, after we had brunch John called and asked if I was free to do the test drive. Absolutely I was, so we made our way home after an uncomfortable walk along the beach front where I swear people were pointing and staring.
I don't blame them, in all fairness I am nothing short of colossal.

Or, what is possibly more so the case, is that no fucker really knows I'm preggers, and they can't quite believe their eyes.

Surprisingly, I've managed to keep my pregnancy off Facebook.
I didn't indulge in the obligatory three-month announcement, nor did I follow it up with various photos of scans. I decided to keep it all to myself because sometimes it's just what a girl must do.

So yes, people may find it hard to believe that Lei Lawson is actually up the duff?! After all, they couldn't quite believe it when I got married, let alone now to be seen waddling along the beach front. Ha! Times really have changed!

The test drive was good though.
I have totally fallen in love with John's Suzuki Swift and even have a name for her. Can I just ask, how the fuck do I have a name for my new car already but after 8 months of searching I still can't find a name for baby Sausage?
Barış that's why.
That fucker says no to every name I pass his way.
Don't get me wrong, he is not forcing me to choose a Turkish name or anything like that. Actually, we have decided that we will give baby Dotty a nice neutral Turkish middle name (which I said he could choose all on his own) but the fucker still won't agree to any of mine. I mean it's not as if they are exactly outlandish now are they?

And then we come to the weekend.
Saturday, other than going food shopping, I did little else other than watch the start of the X Factor. Fuck me, that must mean Christmas is around the corner!

Ahh, our first Christmas with baby Blanket. And the olds will be here too as they have decided that they are coming over for 2 and a half months this year.

2 and a half months.

2. And. A. Half. Months!

How T actual F am I going to cope?
Remember last year and that was only a month!!

Thankfully, Mum suggested that they move to an apartment for the second part of their stay, and although I felt bad agreeing - agree I did none the less.
I know it will be a totally different experience to last year, and I will probably need all hands-on deck, but still – we all need our space, especially me, a girl who spends the majority of time on her own with a TV that doesn't answer back...

So, for today, that's me done.

I have to shift my butt and clean this house which is totally a pain in the arse these days what with it now taking 2 hours opposed to the usual 1, however, sitting down every 5 minutes has become a total necessity.
Then the plan is to retire to the sofa and probably have a little nap.
I have a busy week coming up, so this pregnant wannabe skinny gal needs all the rest she can get.

Oh bloody bastard, I forgot about my promise of sex!
I have done brilliantly in dodging it all week however Husbando has told me in no uncertain terms that he can't last a day longer and seeing as though I am perfectly able to do the sex then tonight is the night.
You would think he would appreciate the fact that I have downloaded him some prime porn to keep him going, but oh no, the selfish fuck wants the real fucking deal - whilst watching the porn!

You can't have it all mate.
You can't have it all…

What a cunt.
Sex. Cankles. Cleaning. And of course me.

Sunday 10th September, 2017
Week 33
Time: 11.32am

Dear Miscreant seeker,

Well well well, I have just had a look at the calendar and it seems I am T–minus 6 weeks till I drop my sprog. How's about that then? Mind you, it's so confusing working out how many months pregnant one happens to be as one app tells me I am 8.5 months and another 7.5.
So, which is it?

Apparently, you can actually hit 10 months if you go through to 43 weeks gestation (fuck knows what that word means), but can you imagine being 10 months pregnant? Jesus, that would be horrific!

All I know is that I have a month and a half to go, so I assume I'm 7.5 months, right?
Unless of course, you don't actually give birth bang on month 9 and it's right at the end of that month?
Confusing.com

I have also been told to expect the arrival of baby Tree any time from week 37 onwards but could also go as far as week 41. But if she has not arrived by then they will induce me.
Poor little sod, being smoked out in such a fashion...
But the issue is she is a big bugger, bigger than she is supposed to be (and yet still no pregnancy diabetes), and I really don't feel like pushing a 4-kilo baby out of my minjeeta. Christ, my downstairs will look like I've had work done by the Krays, slit from arsehole to twat. It really is a good thing a caesarean will be scheduled if baby Butterball gets to 4 kilos then isn't it?!

So urm yeah, fuck alone knows when this baby will put in an appearance, but it's slightly too much for my head to bear on a far too hot for this time of year Sunday morning.

Ahh yes, Sunday morning has made its way round again...

I'm getting used to waking up early with no hangover. In fact, it's not all bad waking up without alcohol sweats and a misty mind. It took some getting used to, but by Jove I think I've got it! That won't stop me from opening up my winter stash of duty free booze that I've been collecting once I am a human lighter; oh no, party time is a comin' – in approximately 4-8 weeks!

So just what has this pregnant fairy been up to this week?
Quite a lot for a change, starting with Monday evening when Sandie and I went into town for a bite to eat and a nosey in the baby shops. You will never guess who walked into 'Yilmaz' restaurant while we were in... Only bloody Lorraine and friend! She could see us from the corner, well before entering, so why choose to continue to the same joint as us? If the roles had been reversed I would most certainly have changed my venue. I mean why put yourself needlessly in that situation?
And to make matters worse, she made a point of standing right by our table discussing with her twin, sorry I mean friend, where they should sit, then decided to sit directly behind us when the restaurant was pretty much empty!

66-year-old psycho alert...!

Now you may wonder if she had actually clocked us, and you wouldn't be wrong to wonder considering – alas, she most definitely saw us as she said hello to Sandie on the way in, which totally flummoxed Sandie as Lorraine usually ignores her...!

And what about this new twinny she has got herself then eh? I couldn't believe my eyes when I saw 2 Lorraine's, all dressed up like it was 8pm and they were dining at the posh end of town.
But no, it was 5pm and 'Yilmaz' – the cheapest little Turkish eatery around for miles...

Anyway, as she had never heard it from my mouth, she may very well not know that I'm with child. So, while we were leaving I made a

point of flaunting my big ole belly in her direction, you know, just for fun.
Sandie said she did a double take.
If she really had no idea before now, then I'm sure as shit she will be shocked that I have not made contact, considering how I used to batter her head about getting pregnant.

Ha! That's dedication for you.

You see, when I'm done, I'm done. I give people far too many chances than they usually deserve, but I do snap eventually, and when I do there ain't no going back – hence why I deleted her back in June. I simply knew this time that I did not want that woman back in my life. Although she did have from January through till June to get in touch should she have wanted too. Nose, spite, face and all that…

Don't get me wrong, sometimes I think it's a shame as we were friends for such a long time, but there is only so much nastiness and sly digs a wannabe socialite can take!

And so, we have both moved on; she quite clearly with a friend of her own age (for once), and me quite clearly with baby.

Sandie and I had a great evening though.
We visited loads of baby shops and I found some black funky baby outfits! Sandie said that they were possibly for boys but that didn't faze me one little bit as I like black, I like rock, and one of the outfits was black with 'born to rock' emblazoned on the front. Plus, I heard this week that 'John Lewis' is going gender neutral for baby clothes, so this has put my mind at ease as boy's clothes are so much funkier than girls.
Please don't misunderstand me 'Dear Diary', I'm not going to force baby Joanie into wearing boys gear at the age of 3 etc, but while she is a tiny little baby, I'm going to have some fun playing dress up the Lei Lawson way.
Gothic rock baby here we come!

Wednesday was another good day.

Barış and I started the afternoon off with a baguette in 'Yunus', then dropped Kastro off to be valeted as she was looking a bit worse for wear, and I couldn't really advertise her for sale in such a state.
It's obviously not something I want to do, sell Kastro, however I can't very well have 2 cars when I don't have the mansion and garage to house them yet. But as soon as I have my rich and famous lifestyle I shall buy Kastro right back and set about pimping her out because she is part of my family and deserves to stay so.
Hello attachment issues.

While she was getting cleaned up we went into town to purchase some Tupperware boxes as bastard weevils had got in my food cupboards again and I needed a way to get rid of the sneaky little suckers for good.
God, I hate weevils.
Why is it every sodding summer they always descend upon *my* cupboards? It's not like my storage areas are filthy dirty – absolutely not, they get a good clean out once a month, so it perplexes me that these little fuckers still come back! Hopefully no more after the Tupperware boxes start doing their job. I just hope that the little shit bags can't eat through plastic like they can cardboard!

Anyway, Kastro was like a new car when I went to collect her, and considering the price (25tl), I don't know why I didn't bother with valeting sooner!

That night I put her on all the stuff for sale pages on Facebook and immediately got phones calls, messages and comments.
But WTF is wrong with people?
When stating NO OFFERS in caps, why are these mo fo's still trying to beat me down from 13,000tl to 10,000 tl!? One buyer even showed up unannounced at 10.30pm at night demanding a test drive and a discount! How the fuck did he even know where we live? Creepy!

Off you fuck - cheeky cunt, that's not the way Lei Lawson does business!

Then on Thursday I did something very out of character. I met a girl (for ease sake let's call her Lisa), that I didn't know and had lunch with her.

Lisa had posted on one of the expat pages that she was new in town, had no friends, and were there were any meet ups or activities to get to know people. Marmaris is not that sort of resort and meet ups are few and far between in the summer as everyone is working.

Me being me I felt a bit sorry for her, and after checking out her Facebook profile I decided that I would meet her. She looked normal enough, in my age bracket and didn't have crazy eyes. However, as life would have it, not one of my brightest ideas.

The conversation did not run smoothly, in fact it was like trying to get blood out of a stone. I found myself chatting shit just to stop the deathly silence. I also had to eat alone because she said that eating in front of others made her feel awkward. Eating alone makes me feel awkward, but this fat mamajamma had no option as baby Grow demanded feeding.

But I don't get it though, why suggest lunch when she knew she wouldn't actually be having lunch?

I find myself saying once again, WTF is wrong with people?

I'm sure the girl is not bad really, but that's something that I will never find out as I don't plan to make the same mistake twice.

But can someone please tell me, where are all the miscreants of this world? Where are the souls on fire? It seems like banter and craik are a rare find in these 'ere parts, and fuck you Lacie for leaving me alone!

So yes, you could say that the friend interview went tits up.
Back to the drawing board is it then.

Luckily Kimmy surprised me with a call on Friday night asking if I was free on Saturday. It's a shame to admit, but my Saturday was wide open...

So, we did the usual and brunched at 'Çinar' then on to 'Starbucks' for treats.

Unfortunately, the rival gang had the same idea and were sat in 'Starbucks' in all their glory, showing off their coiffed do's and botoxed trout pouts.
Clearly, I don't look great these days what with fuck all fitting me, waddling instead of walking, and the heat causing me to never bother doing anything with my face or hair - but did it really need to be those fuckers that I bumped into?

They all waved a quick 'hi' as we passed, but then I heard a mutter from Larissa - the cheeky bitch had the audacity to whisper "who ate all the pies", and not particularly quietly either! This was followed with a ton of cackling from her bunch of bastards.

I flipped around to find them still mumbling, and unfortunately, I couldn't keep my hormones in check when I retorted with "haven't you bitches seen a pregnant woman before?"
"Not one like you Lei" said Larissa, continuing "we all took care of ourselves while going through the same, so it's a shame you felt the need to come out dressed like Kevin or Perry. And hasn't your gynaecologist told you to keep your body mass in check?"

Oh, how I hate that nasty northern cunt!

And guess what?
The usual happened, and my stupid brain left me dumbfounded with no clever reply to hit back with, so Kimmy dragged me off before I made a fool of myself further.

I wish I could blame baby brain, but let's face the fact here folks, I have never been able to think of a good comeback when needed, especially where Larissa is concerned...

FFS though, I didn't think I looked that shockingly hideous. I was in ripped denim maternity shorts, a black vest top, a red and black checked shirt with cut off sleeves, black baseball cap and trademark oversized dark glasses. I looked quite hipster for a pregnant donkey. Well, I thought I looked alright at least.

Clearly. Fucking. Not!

And as for the 'all the pies' comment, yes, I'm carrying a bit of extra chub; some of it's baby weight, some from the UK holiday, but come the fuck on and give me a break – I am 8 months pregnant (or there about)!

So, here we are again back at Sunday.
This afternoon I have a couple of people coming to look at Kastro (if they show up).
I'm getting increasingly more anxious about selling her to the wrong person. I want her to go to a good home, to someone that will love her and care for her and not treat her simply like a *car*. I want her to go to a person like me that has a weird Husbando and a puppy love soul mutt.

Fuck, I'm talking myself out of selling her here.

Pull yourself together Lei, she is only a car when all said and done.
A car that has seen me through the ups and downs of the last 7 years of life, that has played the exact right tunes for the exact right moments, that has broken down on the way to the dreaded ex's house therefore stopping me from making a fool of myself, and, has pretty much been my best friend.
And then some cheeky shit tries to tell me that my *car* is not worth what I'm asking.
No pal, she's not - she's worth way way more than you could ever fucking imagine...

Saturday 16th September, 2017
Week 34
Weight: 75.10 Kilos – Crap I'm nearly 12 stone!
Time: 13.16pm

Dear Girl on a naming mission,

So, Saturday is upon me and I'm sweating like a fat lass in a Marmaris chav bar. I've just finished cleaning the house, a task that I wish I had not taken on, but at least now that it's finished I get to sit on my ever-increasing crack for a few hours.
Talk about too fing hot and too fing pregnant for this malarkey!

What it's also too hot for is pregnancy sex. Well, I say too hot, but I also mean too uncomfortable and too downright painful.
On Monday night we tried to get it on, we really did, but it simply wasn't to be. All the lube in the world wasn't letting that creature in my vage. Yup, my minge simply said NO, and after 10 minutes of huffing and puffing and rubbing and spitting, it was time to give up the sex ghost.
I felt bad of course, but not bad enough to keep from declaring sex off the table 'till baby Cleo arrives.

I Sister Googled it and found that a lot of women give up sex well before now, so Husbando can't say I didn't give him a mighty good run...!

It's a load off actually; no more getting anxious before doing it, no more Guch digging at the bedroom door trying to save his Mother from a fate worse than death, and no more messy bed...
Well, I say no more messy bed, when actually there is never mess on my bed.
Being the clinical Virgo that I am, I have myself a sex towel that gets draped over the bed before we crack on with the nasty. Not very romantic I know but it's so much easier than washing sheets constantly, and, no fights over who has to sleep in the wet spot – although let's face it, I would win every time.

So – no more sex for Lawson for at least 2 months! Yipeeeeeeee! I feel like all my Christmases' have come at once!
But do I feel guilty? Do I fuck as like!
Who in their right mind would want to be having sex at nearly 9 months pregnant anyway???

My good sex mood has not taken me right through the week though. Oh no, there are many a selfish prick here in the Marms to spoil that...

Due to clearing out the nursery I posted my dining room table and chairs on the 'stuff for sale' pages on Facebook in the hopes that they would sell quickly.
I got quite a few offers; some that I rejected on the spot for being cheeky cunts, and three that I agreed could come around to look.
Let's put it this way, I have been house bound for three days in a row with not one of the fuckers showing up!

Seriously, I'm getting sick of saying this, but what the fuck is wrong with people?

And one of the guys I happen to know personally! He was replying at first, and after a missed appointment we even re-arranged for the following day at 3pm, but then, for the second time, he failed to show.
Now he's not opening my messages.
Rude as.

So, now I face a new issue; what if no one wants to buy my table and chairs? I won't have the room I so desperately need in the nursery. What am I supposed to do then?
This is causing me no end of impending doom that I simply do not need during these last few weeks of gestation (am I even using that word correctly?).
I don't want to accept any of the ludicrous offers made, especially as I was quite rude to all that offered less than half my asking price - but I do need to get rid of the bloody things if I want to make my nursery a lovely serene environment for baby Toe nail.

Damn these mo fo's and their rude assed ways!

On the opposite side of the scale is the selling of Kastro.
I do believe that after interviewing a mountain of possible new owners, I have finally found me a nice lady with whom I can re-home her.

She has various likable qualities that the others did not:
Quality 1) she is British: amongst other things, this means that she understood my sentimental attachment and promised not to rename her.
Quality 2) she was respectful: she did not rip through her like a bull in a china shop pointing out all the things wrong with her.
Quality 3) she did not try to barter me down on the price and paid a deposit up front.

So, as you can see, at least one thing is going right this week.

I need to keep hold of Kastro till the end of the month as John seems to be facing the same issue as me – he is not quite ready to let go of his car either. What a pair we make.
But, as sad as I am to be losing Kastro, I am also super excited about my new wheels.

Anyway, this week has been something of a bore. I haven't done much due to the heat and the fact that I dislike everyone right now, Husbando included.
I think maybe my pregnancy hormones are back? Sometimes I wonder if they ever truly left.

But, non the less the week still happened, so let me give you the low down:

On Monday Sandi came over to help move furniture around in the nursery. To cut a long story short we were unable to do F-all because the dining room table and chairs were still in situ. And well, you know the rest...

On Wednesday Husbando and I had an appointment with the Gynae. Usually my appointments last about 7 minutes as it doesn't take long for an ultrasound plus being told what we already know – I've a fat human growing inside me. Once again, he wanted to know what I'd been eating differently as baby Oxygen was piling on the pounds, and once again I informed him that I've eaten sod all different - but that didn't stop him from scheduling another 2-hour bloody glucose test for the following day!
How many more times do I need to be tested for him to believe that I do not have pregnancy diabetes?!

Daft ole Gynae also sent us up to the delivery suite so I could see where I would be giving birth.
Jesus, this shit's getting real!
What also happened up there was what he called a 'Stress Test' where my belly was hooked up to two monitoring devices that listen to the baby's heartbeat. It was interesting for the first 5 minutes but after 20 it became boring as arse, and I found myself nearly drifting off as the bed was so comfortable. Mind you, this 'ere fatty can just about drift off anywhere these days as all I do is eat and sleep…

Apparently the 'Stress Test' is now to be a weekly occurrence because I've hit a milestone at 34 weeks. So every bleedin' week I'm to haul arse back to the hospital, and every bleedin' week they will scandalously bleed me dry of cash.

Ahh well, at least it will only be for another 6 weeks (or less) …

As we weren't banking on being in the hospital for such a long time, we were both ravenous by the time we made it to 'Yunus' for lunch. Nothing else for it, we ordered a great big fat Turkish breakfast and proceed to stuff our faces.
It filled a hole in my massively increasing appetite.

After our feed we headed down town. I wanted to register with the state clinic for all the after-birth visits as although we have coughed up the cash for pre-natal's at the private hospital, I certainly don't intend to continue there once I have given birth. Alas, we got there

too late and the Doctor had gone, so, I will just have to drag my arse there again this coming week.
As if I've not got enough to do…

Whilst in town I also popped into 'Etcetera' card shop to get a couple of birthday cards, and who should I bump smack bang into? Jess the Minger!
Jesus, I've not seen Jess for over a year, and the last time we bumped into each other it didn't go so well. We were both out with our separate crews and she had a go at me for not inviting her to my wedding. Can I just ask though, why would I invite someone that I'm not speaking to, to my already overcrowded wedding?

This 'bump into' was quite different, in fact it was, dare I say, *pleasant*. I congratulated her on getting married and she congratulated me on the pregnancy. We had a 20-minute chat and when I left I felt at ease with the world.

Actually, it's not the first time I have heard from her recently. She contacted me the minute she found out Sister had died. She was very supportive and even offered to take me to Rhodes for a weekend piss up in his memory. Little did she know then that I was up the duff and couldn't do anything of the sort, but it's the thought that counts.

Thursday morning had me up at the butt crack of dawn to do the stupid glucose test at the hospital. What a waste of two hours that was.
When I called for my results I certainly wasn't shocked to find that I still don't have diabetes and was in the perfectly healthy range. Just a big fat baby, that's all.
Apparently, my butterball weighs in at 2.75 Kilos when she should be around the 2.25 mark, and, her weight is set to double in the coming weeks…
Clearly takes after me then, damn it.

I better be getting a bloody 'push present', that's all I can say…

And that's literally all I've done this week.
Next week is looking very different; in fact, that's when the stress will start, alas, that's next week's problem.

All I need to concentrate on for now is making sure that I don't get harassed with these baby names. Mum keeps asking if we have decided on one, and the short answer to that is no because Barış and I have very different taste. He wants something traditional like Victoria, Margaret or Gökçe, and I, obviously do not.
Yup, mo fo has now started dropping Turkish names in the mix after promising he wouldn't.

It's taking its toll believe me; a happy household we are not.

Even Guch is showing his unhappiness about this situation as he had a little spate of sickness the poor soul. His tummy emulated mine when it trebled in size and I'm not afraid to say that I shit myself with worry.
It took the vet 5 minutes and 180tl to tell me that he was suffering from gas and needed to fart it out. She gave him a couple of injections and a syringe of 'Gaviscon' then sent me on my way. And true to word, Gucci farted it out like a good 'un. The house still stinks now, almost a week later!

Well, I better get off.
I need to squirt nasal spray up my nostrils to unblock my constantly blocked nose that have been blocked since the start of pregnancy. A good solid pick simply doesn't do the trick anymore. Plus, I'm hungry - another symptom that has me looking like the tide should come and collect me.
Talking about food, I'm off to the 'Taj' tonight with Kimmy and her sisters. As lovely as that will be I simply don't know how I'm going to lose this pregnancy weight, and I'm scared...
But that, 'Dear Diary', is a problem for October 26th...

Sunday 24th September, 2017
Week 35
Time: 11.18am

Dear Traumatic turd girl,

Yesterday was September 23rd 2017, and if you were to believe the internet hype, it was supposedly the day of rapture, and, Jesus's second coming.
But which one actually happened?
I'm assuming Jesus as no apocalypse occurred, unless I missed it?

And there I was lounging on the sofa in anticipation while watching 'Donnie Darko' waiting for the world to be hit by wayward planet Nibiru (again), which didn't happen (again).
Talk about a wasted day...

Let's also not forget that I'm the one spawning the next prophet, so if that happens to be you Jesus, you best bide your time – I still have a month left...

So, for now, as all seems well on planet earth, it looks like you're stuck with me. Not that I was convinced the end was nigh of course. I have been through this waiting game before back in 2012, and it didn't happen then either.
Unless it did, and we are all living on the 'Lost' island?

Ooooh, what a thought for a Sunday morning!

All I can say is this – Guch seems alright and he's bound to know the gen, being a direct descendant of God and all.

Mind you, I did wake up with claws this morning and that freaked me out somewhat. Both hands were literally clawed over, with the right hand also suffering from 2 locked fingers.
WT Actual F?
I've just Sister Googled 'locked fingers when pregnant' and apparently, it's a thing come 8 months or so.

Pregnancy carpel tunnel syndrome – that's what I have been gifted with this week.

Due to sausage fingers, I removed my rings about two weeks ago, but that has nothing on this present swell, what with my locked bloody fingers too! I mean whatever next!

I was half convinced that the devil had been a-visiting, but I haven't done a Ouija board since Jen left and I certainly wouldn't now for fear of possession of my unborn baby messiah, so, that's put paid to my visitation theory (I hope) …
Let's just pray my deformed ole claw hands piss off once I've dropped the sprog, because God knows, I wouldn't want to be stuck with these satanic phalanges…

For fucks sake, my imagination gets more ridic' as the days go by.
Pregnancy can be weird man.
Maybe it's because I've had somewhat of a stressful week?

Last weekend wasn't exactly stressful though.
Saturday night consisted of eating my body weight in Indian food at the 'Taj' with Kimmy and Co, then going for a drink in 'The Waterhole' on the beachfront.
The only possibly stressful part about the evening was when I ordered a Fanta and the waiter (whom I had never met before) proceeded to tell me that fizzy drinks were bad for the baby, so I was to have water instead.
Say what now?
Who the fuck did this jumped up little tit of an 18-year-old think he was, preaching to me, someone nearly twice his age?
Cheeky little cunt.

For the love of God, it's not as if I was ordering vodka with my Fanta! That I could understand, but bloody Fanta all on its own?

Of course I didn't listen, I ordered my Fanta, but it put me off staying as paranoia set in leaving me thinking that every fucker in the place was judging me and said Fanta.
This must be what pregnancy shame feels like…
So, I left after that. Not like me to give in so easily, but I really didn't fancy another encounter with the know-it-all waiter.

Question: Why do some folk feel the need to butt in? Especially restaurant/bar staff.
It's not the first time I've had a run in with F&B people and been told what I can and can't drink whilst out, but if Husbando doesn't have a problem with it, then why the fuck should anyone else? His is the only opinion that matters after all, and his opinion is 'let the Lawson drink what she damn well pleases'.
Quite right too.

Anyway, on Sunday our little group continued with the food overload with a Turkish breakfast at 'Çinar'.
Before pregnancy, the only way I would have been able to fit that amount of grub in my belly would be if I was hung-over. And let's face it, on a Sunday morning I would have been just that. But now? Well, I can fit in that and more! I am just so hungry all the time! Sister G said that by this week I shouldn't be able to fit as much in because baby Button will be squashing my tummy.
But Sister G lied.
And, I went on to order a great big pizza from 'Dominoes' for my dinner.

To be completely honest, I am ashamed of my glutinous self.
In the last month my eating has trebled, as have my chubby cheeks. My legs that are usually a bit on the scrawny side have beefed right up and don't even look like they belong to me. I can't comment on what my stomach looks like because for now there is a baby living in it, but by Christ, once that baby's out I wonder just what sort of state I will be left with?

I see Sister's prophecy was right; pregnant me has blown up like a sodding blow fish. I just pray that some of this chub is water retention 'else I'm fucked.

So yes, maybe a food overdose and a jumped up li'l wank stain, but not a particularly stressful weekend...

Oh, and I finally managed to sell my dining room table and chairs! The lady who bought them bartered Barış down nearly 100tl (the dick), but there was F-all I could do about it as I was out at the time. At least they are out of the way leaving me to have loads of fun arranging baby Neptune's nursery.
It looks brill by the way, and I think it's fair to say I'm pretty pleased with myself. It's not a very babyish nursery as that's not what I like, but it is all white and pristine with just the odd flash of teddy bear here and there.

Yes, I'm going to be very happy spending time in that room, especially with the new curtains that I bought on Monday when I went into town with Sandi.

We had a good rake though the readymade curtains and decided on a funky floral purple set. Anything purple works for me, after all, that room's colour scheme was various shades of purple before it was stripped of all things Lei.
We also had a nose in the craft shop. I want to make something myself you see, to personalise the room a little bit, but without having a name to work with it makes life just that little bit harder...
Damn you Barış with your shitty name ideas!

But a nice afternoon we had, and thankfully this time we didn't bump into Lorraine, although I spotted Larissa with one of the rival gang in my favourite clothes shop 'Ambar'.
You will never believe what she was doing...!? While being videoed by butt plug gang member, Larissa was trawling through clothes and talking directly to the camera, 'a la ITV's 'Trinny Woodall'.
How fucking extra.
I mean who the fuck does she really think she is?

As queen bitch is still on my Facebook, curiosity got the better of me and I found myself seeking out said video later that day.
Oh cringe – fucking cringe.
Doesn't she realise what she looks like?
What an absolute wanker!
I wonder where she gets such a high opinion of herself when a few years ago she looked like she could do with a bloody good scrub with soap and water?

Reading through the comments on the video made me physically sick.
Her little gang of turd worms were unashamedly crawling up her arsehole telling her to make a career out of this lunacy.

OH PLEASE FUCK OFF!

This was simply too much for me to bear, and for two whole minutes I actually considered deleting her arse. Just for two minutes though.

Wednesday could have been where the stress started.
We had to be in Mugla at the butt crack of dawn for my residency renewal appointment as I stupidly booked it for 9am. It's never an easy task getting up at 06.30am, especially as I usually sleep till 10am, and what with Barış not being a morning person it made for a difficult start.

Surprisingly Barış kept his morning attitude at bay. Maybe because I had warned him for the last 3 days that I didn't want to encounter nasty Barış on residency renewal day 'cos that shit is stressful enough already.
Fair play, he was golden and even treated me to a 'Burger King' when we got back to Marmaris.

Wednesday afternoon was spent at my hospital check-up. Would you believe it, my 'Stress Test' showed that I was having actual contractions!

The Gynae asked several times if I could feel anything, but no, all I could feel was a bit of period pain. He jumped on this immediately and asked how long I had the period feeling, and when I said a day or so, he told me off for not coming in sooner.
How was I supposed to know that period pain is what contractions feel like?!

As it was clear that I was definitely not in labour, he sent me packing to come back on Friday (unless my waters broke in-between) for another 'Stress Test'.
So off I went with a flea in my ear and a comforting feeling of being instructed to do as little as possible. What a welcome thought that was after a stressful Wednesday...

Thursday, I did indeed do what the Gynae told me. Although I desperately needed to go food shopping, I fought the urge to leave the house and instead Sister Googled labour pains versus Braxton Hicks. As the period pain had disappeared, I'm assuming it's a spot of the Toni's I was having.

I swear to God, I never knew contractions would feel like period pain.
In fact, for some strange reason, I never wondered what the start of labour would feel like at all. I automatically assumed I would just know.
Clearly bloody not...!

Friday, I cancelled my Turkish lesson as I wanted to get to the hospital as early as possible seeing as though baby Cash could soon be on her way. The test showed all was back to normal – no more contractions. Apparently, they were probably caused by stress or overdoing it. That's all I needed to hear – hello sofa and reality TV, my two best friends.

But just before retiring to the sofa for the rest of my pregnancy, I celebrated with Kate and cake at the new patisserie in Armutalan, 'Hemşin'.

I hadn't clapped eyes on Kate for about a month because I was totally avoiding her. Wrong I know, but I was scared that she had become my worst fear, so I played the dodge game. Thankfully, the know-it-all attitude wasn't as present as it was the last time we met, and we had a nice enough arvo, but, through no fault of her own, Lacie she is not.

I'm feeling some teenage angst towards that Lacie at the moment. She should be here with me during this pregnancy instead of sunning herself, this week in Mexico. Every photo she sends gets me angrier and angrier. Here I am in bloody Marmaris living a life far too ordinary for a wannabe socialite, and there she is, living the life of an actual socialite...
What the F is going on man?
How have I ended up with no Marmaris bestie and a body that looks like it belongs to a sumo wrestler?
Well, it wasn't through sitting on some fucker's face now was it...

And then we come to Saturday – the night that brought about the most traumatic turd experience of my life.

All day long I had been suffering with blood red snotters, something that I've gotten used to over the last 8 months, but that wasn't a patch on the vileness of just what I was about to experience...

It started out with the feeling of needing a poo. Nothing abnormal about that right?

As my poo's have gotten less frequent and harder to push out, I sat and let it percolate for a while, making sure that it was absolutely ready to flop right out by the time I sat on the bog.
But nope, it wasn't to be.

I was sat on that loo screaming in agony, trying to push that monster out for no less than 25 minutes. At one point I thought fuck this and squeezed it back up, wiped, flushed, and was about to sit on the sofa before the rip-roaring pain was driven back down through my anus and forced me back to the toilet for another 15 minutes.

Barış was beside himself. He had no idea what to do and kept suggesting that we go to the hospital to get it forcefully removed. Yeah alright man, I will just get dressed, go to the hozzy and endure the humiliation of having them remove a turd the size of Gucci from my arsehole, abso-fucking-lutely.

No, Lei Lawson takes a challenge head on.

So, I asked Barış if he wouldn't mind taking a look instead, and if he could just grab hold of the fucker and pull it out, then all the better for my torn-up crack.
The horrified look on his face told me that this was not going to happen.
Bloody cowardice Judas.

So, I did what any wannabe socialite could, gave myself a stern talking to and pushed through the pain.

Finally, after what I can only describe as the worst experience of my life, the monster turd had freed itself from the grasp of my arse cheeks.

That was some bastard pain let me tell you, and after examining the article I'm not sodding surprised. You should have seen the size of the thing - it was fucking HUGE! Not just length ways but width ways too, in fact the width of the monster was the most shocking of all!
Seriously, I'm surprised I don't need stitches after that mother fucker clawed itself out.
And I swear that alien turd was winking at me while its 2-kilo self made its way to the bottom of the bog, because a floater it was not!

I shall remember that experience 'till the day I die, which won't be long if I have to go through that again.

And now?

Well, it's time to flush that memory and retire to the sofa. After all, my feet are swollen (as is my arse), I'm hungry and I fancy some TV binging.

Fuck Larissa and fuck ginormous turds.

OCTOBER

Sunday 1st, 2017
Week 36
Weight: 76 Kilos – Yup, 12 stone has hit
Time: 11.09am

Dear Dripping anal glands,

Yipeee, the weather has finally cooled to where I am no longer leaving patches of piss sweat wherever I sit. I am instead dealing with patches of asshole stainage, but more about that later.
At least there are actual clouds in the sky!
#SmallMercies

I love this time of year because I can finally put my face on without it sliding right off, and I can wear my hair down without feeling like I'm about to die, or, look like a big frizzy yeti - something which hasn't happened since May!

Yup, life is nearly all good in Lei's world right now, and it's all down to this glorious weather! Well, it wouldn't be down to the bloody anal stains now would it…

Pregnancy wise all looks well too. As if on cue, I have started to get the back twinges that Sister Google promised come week 36. That coupled with the occasional period pain is apparently Braxton Hicks at its finest.
It's both an interesting yet daunting feeling getting these false contractions as it means that the body is getting ever ready to push baby Megan out, and, I can say with all honesty, that I don't think I'm quite ready for her. Yes, the nursery is pretty much done, but head space wise, I need more time.

At the start of the diary I seem to recall mentioning that I was so obsessed with getting pregnant that it didn't cross my mind what it would be like to in fact have baby Easy Jet in the here and now. And now that it's about to happen, I'm pretty sure that I'm still taking things too lightly.
I find myself far too chilled about it all, surely I must be forgetting something, right?

Even when I half packed my hospital bag on Thursday, I can honestly say it didn't hit home that it's me that's giving birth soon. More like I was packing for a friend.
Weird eh?
Husbando on the other hand saw the little suitcase in the nursery and freaked the fuck out. He was all like "who's that for" and "OMFG there's a baby in your belly".
Well duh…

Mind you, it's not as if either of us have a clue what to do with a baby, so let's just hope that my olds make it in time, otherwise I will be stuck with the dreaded M-I-L who I have not seen since we got wed 2.5 years ago!

Barış is a bit odd when it comes to his family. He believes they should be kept at an arm's length, so I guess I'm kind of lucky as we don't have them dropping by constantly like some of my friends.

For me, it's more of a language barrier that stops me from inviting M-I-L here more often. We simply have no idea what the other is saying, and that 'Dear Diary' is literally Google translation torture.

Sister never could translate a paragraph well after all…

So how the hell can Mum speak 7 bloody languages and I can't seem to get a grasp of sodding Turkish after living here for 20 years?
This can't be normal.
Clearly, I'm just a simpleton.
Must take after my Dad then… But he's no simpleton either. Go figure.

Anyway, as far as M-I-L's go she is an all alright sort; she doesn't butt in with our lives, she doesn't make a nuisance of herself, and due to the language barrier I don't even have to speak to her all that often, but there is one major problem when she does come to visit - she refuses to be in the house if Gucci is in situ, and as it's Gucci's house, he's always going to be in situ.
So, what happens is that she demands that Guch live on the balcony while she is in the vicinity and that simply doesn't work for me.
This happened once while I went to the UK for my usual summer escape and she came to visit Barış for a week. He didn't tell me 'till half way through her holiday about what was going on, and at that point I took an eppy fit and kicked off. No way was my boy living on the balcony to accommodate a woman that claims to like dogs but won't have one anywhere near her.

So, from half the world away I informed Barış that if his Mother couldn't cope with Gucci in the house then she was to get a hotel, as from that precise point onwards, Guch was back indoors.

Needless to say, I was called all cunts under the sun when she cut short her holiday and left the very next day, but, that's none of my business…

Anyway, I've had a busy week waddling around, so I best get to telling you about it;

On Monday I did one of my least favourite things and that was to visit the bank. I needed to take some cash out for the new car so it's not as if it could be avoided. It went smoother than I thought, and I left feeling OK for a change.

Mind you, since moving banks at the beginning of the year I do find it a lot less stressful and I no longer get spoken down to. Honestly, it used to be a harrowing experience visiting my old bank - the way they speak to 'Yabanci's' (us foreign lot) is simply appalling. No customer service and they don't give a shit about managing your money as being a foreigner you simply aren't worth the hassle.

Awful really how they get away with it, hence why I moved banks once my Mother experienced it first hand and told me I deserved better.

Quite right too Mum!

On the way home, I decided to call in on Sandi and force her to feed me, which God love her she did, and I didn't even have to ask! She's a good un, like an aunty to me I suppose. Not at all uptight like Lorraine used to get when I saw my other friends. Sandi knows that the world doesn't revolve around her because she is normal, and normal is exactly what I need in my life right now.

I spent a lovely two hours there and then took myself off home to walk Guch.

Tuesday was an odd one.

Guch wasn't his normal self so instead of going out for lunch I decided to have a home day with him instead. I'm glad I did because he was like a little lost lamb. He wasn't jumping on the sofa, bed, or up at me when he saw the lead for walkies, then his back went all hunched and his face all scrunched. And when Barış came home from work, Guch bit him on the nose.

I - of - course Sister Googled all of this, but I didn't need Sister G to realise that my poor wee soul was sick...

So, back to the vets we went, at 10.30pm.

Alev my vet is great *when* she answers the phone. She didn't think twice about opening the surgery for Guch, after all, she has known him since he was just a little pup, and, she loves cash.

Turns out my poor boy had a bit of a tummy infection dating back to when he had gas last week, so more Gaviscon, more injections, and of course, more cash.
It worked at least, and Guch slept soundly on the bed cuddled up next to me that night.

On Wednesday we were up an at it early doors, after all, I had cars to buy and sell! But before the buying and selling began, Husbando and I decided to take Kastro out on one last run to 'Asparan' and treated ourselves to a great big breakfast.
The breakfast was bittersweet, and I don't mind admitting that I pretty much sobbed all the way back to Marms knowing I was to lose my best friend shortly thereafter.

All I can say is I'm a big fat traitor.

After all the paperwork was done and I jumped in Suzette the Swift, I didn't think twice about Kastro.
Oh how I enjoyed driving a pretty much new car for the first time in years! I felt like the Queen with my new wheels. The radio wasn't hanging out of its hole, the air con worked, the dash board was like a digital dream, and, I could control the music from the steering wheel! I was as happy as a pig in shit.

Sorry Kastro, you have been replaced...

As you can imagine, Thursday and Friday were spent cruising in Suzette, getting a feel for her and being a car wanker by testing out the sound system. I have the feeling that baby Neck Brace likes Inxs. Well, she booted me pretty hard when I had myself a long loud screech-a-long, so that's a good sign.

Friday brought with it the brown arse oil leakage, but let me just point out that for once, it didn't belong to me...!
My dear sweet Guch is really going through the mill this week, as now, on top of his infection, he is dropping anal gland oil sporadically throughout the house. In the last few weeks this has

happened 3 times, however it was only on Friday that I realised it wasn't wee.

Yup, while he was sat next to me on the sofa being petted whilst watching 'TOWIE', he leaked.
That just goes to show what he thinks of that programme then eh!
I checked him over to find that it certainly wasn't coming from his wiener - nope, this was all his anal glands, and FML it wasn't pretty. And what a fucking stench!

I fetched the wet wipes immediately and cleaned my boy up, then got on to phone the vet to ask what should be done.
Nothing apparently as it's normal…
Well I disagree – Guch has only recently started doing this, never in his life has he done so before - so normal it most certainly is not!

Yes, he's had to have his anal sack manually emptied before (obvs not by myself because eww gross) but leaking around the house is a first. And it's on a different level of grimness entirely to a piss fest, as that doesn't leave brown arse oil stainage all over.

Clearly, I am not going to put up with this so, guess what – more cash to be thrown at the vet...

On Saturday I had a late lunch with Vicky the diehard party animal. She is back in town for two weeks so naturally I wanted to have a catch up. Unfortunately, it couldn't be done whilst on a booze bender, so we had to do it over a baguette and chips instead.

On the walk down to the 'Maris Beach' hotel where we were having lunch, a guy that I have known for 20 odd years, who works at the beach front water park, stopped us for a chat. He didn't know I was pregnant so was shocked to see me ready to drop.
He is usually a lovely chap so when he informed me that the baby had 'eaten' my beauty and I was one ugly female at 9 months pregnant, I honestly thought he was taking the piss. Who wouldn't right?

Then he went on to tell me that after giving birth and going on a severe diet that it shouldn't take too long for my beauty to return. So, he was serious then!?

What the actual fuck?
Was this fucker on crack?

After the initial shock wore off, my mind kicked into action and he got a mouthful that went along the lines of: "How very dare you, you shouldn't speak to a pregnant woman like that as some of us already feel rather shit about ourselves, and you pointing it out in front of other people is simply cruel. I suggest that you keep your shitty mouth shut, and in future never ever say this to another pregnant woman again, you absolute inconsiderate arsehole you".

Fucker took it all in his stride didn't he, and stated that usually, instead of getting an ear bashing, women usually thank him for his comments. I can't imagine why, and I told him so. He went on to say that we have known each other for 20 years and I shouldn't be upset as my beauty will return in a couple of months.
Then he tried to high five me.

Urm?
I know Turks never have been backward in coming forward, but come on...

I'm quite surprised that I was able to restrain myself from chinning the cunt because that's exactly what the 5 foot nothing little fuckwitt deserved...

And I hate to admit it but that little arse-face got in my head and subsequently lunch was tarnished because I couldn't get his comments out of my mind. I couldn't help but wonder if every person that I bumped into happened to think the same?

Cheers fucktard. You have pretty much ruined what pregnancy confidence I have left. But be careful Max, I've marked your cards and I've been known to dabble in sorcery!

So, after what seems like a long week, I'm going to push his comments to the back of my mind and rest up the cankles while watching TV for an hour. After that I will make work of swapping my summer clothes for my winter wardrobe that has been living under the spare room bed for the last 6 months.
It's actually a bit early for the winter swap, but I know that if I leave it much longer this hideous pregnant creature will no longer have the will nor motivation to do so... Plus, I need to pull my finger out and get that bedroom parents ready.

Oh, and P.S: Jenny finally got a reply from the Turkish consulate and her ban has been lifted! Yipeeeee – My friend is soon to be on her merry way!

Sunday 8th October, 2017
Week 37
Time: 11.11am

Dear (Day) dream believer,

Early mornings seem to have become a habit for this 'ere sloth of late, with today being no exception. I thought I may be due a bit of a lie in due to a massive storm last night holding my slumber hostage, alas, the lie in didn't happen.
I must say I found it quite comforting lying in bed listening to the rain hammer down around me for the first time since May. It gave me that tingly winter feeling that I just adore.
And all without so much as a sheet to cover the colossus that is my body because it's too damn hot still!

So why didn't I take the lie in considering it's Sunday after all?
Well, I couldn't tell what time it was as every sodding clock in the house has stopped and I had no idea if it was my usual waking hour or not.
Wouldn't it have been a coincidence if all the clocks stopped at the same time? That could have been considered some sort of witchcraft, but no – plain and simply laziness is all.

The first of the 4 clocks stopped about 4 years ago and now simply sits in the nursery as decoration. The second stopped (I want to say) in May, with the third stopping about a month ago, and the fourth – the most important one as it's our bedroom clock - stopped just last night.

As I stupidly keep my mobile in the lounge, I had to get up to turn it on, and when I finally did, I found it was only 07.20am.
What a stupid fool.
I should have known it was a bit too dark outside to be my get up time, but as it was stormy and dark anyway, I really can't be to blame for this foolishness.

So, as I was up and about and my eyes had adjusted to being somewhat awake, I decided to watch some mindless TV to see if that would induce a nap on the sofa for at least an hour.
That didn't happen because I chose the least boring thing ever to watch: 'The People vs OJ Simpson'. Oh yes, I got right into it. Four episodes later and I could barely tear myself away from the screen to make this diary entry.
In fact, I find myself rushing just so I can get back to it.

Funny how you can get addicted to something so quickly isn't it?

I used to be like that with certain blokes, addicted quickly I mean. Some fella's just have the 'X Factor' that get my obsession brewing from the offset.
Remember the Dentist...?
In his case the 'X Factor' certainly wasn't looks, not with his floppy mop of slicked back hair, evil black eyes and wonky teeth. Not a very good advertisement for a dentist really, but the fucker got me every time.
What he had was more dangerous than good looks – he had the *bad boy* attitude that I couldn't get enough of. You know, the 'treat 'em mean, keep 'em keen' vibe.
Fuck sake, he had it down to a fine art.

I wonder if it would work now if I was still a single wannabe socialite instead of this married ole chunk?
Interesting thought, but not one I'm going to waste much time thinking about.

Instead let me tell you about my crazy arsed dreams that have been ramped-up a notch in the last few weeks.
On pregnancy forums, mums to be often mention their fucked-up dreams, but they ain't got nothing on me. I have fucked up dreams pregnant or not, but in the last 3 to 4 weeks they have gone from being simply fucked up to 'Lei needs to be sectioned'.
I am lucky that in most cases the need to wee wakes me up, because if I had to stay in some of them for much longer I think I might actually die.

They say that's a real thing you know, if you die in your dream you die in real life too. And what a way I would go - the monster that looks like a toaster who is renowned for killing fairies gas chamber style is finally about catch me, and sometimes, in another dream entirely, my wings disappear mid-flight and I am about hit the deck from 20 stories up.

My dreams are so real that sometimes when I wake, I occasionally fear for Barış's safety. Some dreams you see, happen to involve me coming home from a hard day's work to find his face buried in a faceless female's crotch, and I proceed to murder the filthy bastard right there.
Sometimes this is done with my bare hands, and sometimes I strangle the cheating mother fucker with his own willy.

Thank God they are just dreams because an anaconda cock I neither want nor need.

So yes, my over active mind is dreaming up a frenzy these days. I suppose I should be mighty thankful that no birthing nightmares make it through.
Maybe my sub-conscious is looking after me and taking my mind off the immanent with all the near-death crap - unless of course, that's a sign? Or maybe, I'm still super chilled out about it all and my sleeping self feels no need to be concerned?
And at 37.5 weeks pregnant who would have thunk it?!

Anyway, this week has been somewhat of a social one, not that I have looked the part. I now have only 3 tops that I can wear, and wearing them in rotation is getting me down.
I can't wait to be able to don my normal wardrobe again - I just wonder how long it will take before I'm able to?
Hopefully with the diet coffee that I've ordered I should be back to my usual 63.5 kilo self in a couple of months max, but I do fear that with having the olds here for 2.5 months, not much dieting is going to take place.
Damn me and my love for food!

Anyhow – back to my week;
So, Monday I went into town with Sandi. We seem to do a lot of that of late. One of the reasons is because on those days I don't have to cook for myself as we always eat out, and God knows I can't be arsed to stand in the kitchen for long at the moment.

Mind you, I always seem to spend a fortune on a load of shit when we do head to town. Take Monday for example; we hit up the craft shop again as I am still in the mood for making a wall decoration for the nursery. What would possibly have cost me 2 or 3 lira in the lira shop, cost me 25 in the craft shop, but I was adamant that I wanted to make the wall deco all on my own.
So basically, I fleeced myself.
Stupid cow...

I did however, find a lovely lilac fleecy throw for the nursery sofa that didn't break the bank, and, a baby bouncer that Guch has already tried out. In fact, he is in the nursery now trying to get back onto it the silly sod.

Then came Tuesday when I went to visit Connor Candlish and co. Yup, Connor and his ever-ready schlong are back in town for a week, and, he bought with him some duty free for when I've popped.
What a thoughtful angel.

Unfortunately, I couldn't join in with their pissed-up antics, but being pregnant certainly did save me from their love of chav bars... I did however spend an interesting afternoon with them at the 'Laberna' hotel, and I even treated myself to a shandy which I had to send back twice as I swear there was zero sprite in it and I could feel a buzz after 2 gulps!
God, what am I going to be like the first time I have a real drink? Pissed after a glass of voddie - whatever next?!

On Wednesday it was up at the butt crack of dawn as we had to go back to Mugla, this time to register Suzette the Swift. I despise early

mornings and the people that force them upon me, so needless to say I wasn't happy about having to go...
Why oh why these things can't be done in Marmaris is bloody well beyond me. Oh yes, I know why – because I'm a bloody foreigner! Talk about having us jump through hoops...

We set off at 07.15am, stopping en route at the bakery for brekky, making it to Mugla police station for 08.45am.
I would like to say that it was a smooth process of registration, and that all was done within half an hour - but that would be a blatant lie. Yes, we were only in the police station for 30 odd minutes, but that was because they wouldn't accept my residency (as it had run out), nor would they accept the document from the residency office that was supposed to replace my expired residency and work in place of the new one.
Bunch of bastards.

They went on to inform us that we needn't have come to Mugla as they stopped this procedure for Yabanci's last year, and that we could now register the car in our local cop shop in Marms.

Well thank you for the wasted trip you stupid people in the notary office that informed us this was a must! That cost me half a tank of petrol, three hours of sleep and a day of needless carb loading!

And you just know what's going to happen when my new residency does arrive and we try to register Suzette in the Marmaris cop shop, don't you? We will be sent back to fucking Mugla - that's what!
As if I was not worried enough about driving an hour out of town at 37 weeks preggers anyway, now they will have me doing it while in labour!

After that fiasco, it was just my luck that we had another Gynae appointment to get too.
Jesus, my life is so rock 'n' roll...

And just what morsels of wisdom did the Gynae have to say for himself this week?

Well, I'm having contractions again aren't I.
I still don't feel these contractions, however they are happening whether I feel them or not. So, I was sent away and told to cross my legs as it's not quite time for baby Narnia to come out just yet.
At least he didn't schedule another appointment to repeat the 'Stress Test' this week, because that I fear, would have tipped me over the edge.

On Thursday I had somewhat of a less stressful day.
I binge watched 'Liar' and completed phase 2 of getting the winter wardrobe out from under the bed. Nothing else to report other than I kept my swollen fat trotters up for the majority of the day.
Gucci enjoyed the company and I enjoyed chilling with Guch.
#HappyTimes.

Friday was spent between my Turkish lesson and 'Migros'. I never usually shop at 'Migros' as it's one of the more expensive supermarkets in Marmaris, however 'Kipa' was closed due to it being converted into 'Carrefour', so, I had no bloody choice.
As much as I dislike 'Kipa' at times, it is always more preferable than going to 'Migros' where I don't know where anything is, and my bill was over 50tl for 4 small bags of fruit.
Thieving gits.

Saturday was a better day.
I picked up Kate and we hit 'Şahin Tepe' for brunch. We chatted about all kinds of shite; how our Husbando's drive us mental, how life in Marms is simply ridiculous, the drama of the ex-pats, and Facebook wars.

Yup, there have been more, and this time all because a tourist had posted on a group that her son was offered drugs in a bar. She was only giving people a general warning - nothing wrong with that right? Wrong!

Oh this poor woman – she was branded a liar, a shit stirrer, a gob shite and a cunt – all for warning folk! Oh yes, the tourist mafia were out in full force because their 'favourite' bar where *they* had never been offered drugs in the last 10 years had been tarnished.

Just because it has never happened to you Susan, doesn't mean it hasn't happened.

I hate to repeat myself, but what the fuck is wrong with people?

There was even this one bloke that said he was on the way down to the bar to inform the manager of this 'slander' and to leave it in the hands of the Turks. I mean come the fuck on David, give yer head a wobble…

The woman ended up deleting her post for fear of the unknown. I don't blame her after the volume of abuse she received, which mostly happened to be from my fair countrymen!

She said she won't come back to Turkey, and that's a shame. It's not because her son got offered drugs as she is fully aware that happens everywhere in the word – nope, this was because of the vile messages and comments.
And that's the real shame.

So that's where I'm going to leave you for today. I need to watch at least one more episode of 'OJ' before I complete the third and final phase of the winter wardrobe saga.
I'm also hungry and feel a face feed coming on. It's 12.57pm now and it will be the fourth time I've eaten so far today.
No wonder I look the way I do….

2 AND A HALF MONTHS LATER

Monday 1st January, 2018
Time: 09.57am

Dear Diary,

Hello old friend, it's been a while.

A massive amount has gone down in the last couple of months, so much so that I simply don't know where to start! So, I'll just to fumble my way through, and if I happen to jumble it all up, just blame it on the mush that is formerly known as Lei Lawson's brain…

So here it is in a nutshell:

Nutshell 1) Lacie is leaving the sugar daddy and making her way home to the Marms, and, it's about damn time too! You will never believe it, but Wannabe popped up from out of nowhere, declared his undying love and put a ring on it.
Jesus, could ole Wannabe be the one for our Lacie after all?
Who would have thunk it!

Nutshell 2) Jenny finally got her arse back to Marmaris for a cheeky week at the beginning of November. Bless her, you could tell she really missed the place. And shock horror, we only went out on the piss the once! What's all that about then?

Well…

Nutshell 3) That's right, I finally dropped my sprog!

Yup, for the last 2.5 months I have been kept super busy with my seven and a half pounder.

In fact, since popping my feet have barely touched the ground! It's been one hell of an emotional rollercoaster, but more of that later as I want to get straight to the point (for once).

Without further ado, I would like to introduce you to baby Lennie Mai. Born 11 days early on 14th October 2017 at 09.55am, after an 18-hour labour.
And, as you can see – no Turkish names in sight! I got my own way, finally.
You may wonder why seeing as though my little dah-ling is a half Turk? Well, other than it was me who carried her for 9 months, and it was also me that pushed a watermelon out of my hoo ha - all will become clear as we continue…

Now which lying bastard proclaimed that time makes you forget the pain of childbirth?
I can tell you right now that time has done nothing of the sort - I still remember each and every brutal detail. Those horrific hours are etched in my brain mush for life. In fact, I think the trauma has left me with PTSD.
Honest.

Every time I think back to that day two things happen:
Thing 1) I wince and my fanny tightens.
Thing 2) Feelings of pure unadulterated hatred towards Barış rise to the surface.

I swear I could have killed him for what he did to me, and I don't just mean knocking me up. But before I divulge the Barış deets, I had better explain just how little Lennie Mai made her Marmaris debut…

Let me take you back to Friday October 13th, 2017 - Picture the scene, if you will;

It was a warm balmy October's day. Warm enough to only be dressed in shorts and a vest top. Although I was nigh on ready to drop, I found myself with pregnancy OCD and cleaned the house from top to bottom, albeit stopping for breath every five minutes. I had even planned on going to see Sandie for a coffee after my final Turkish lesson before the 'big day', but, life had other plans...

So I was making my way to Sandie's from my Turkish lesson, sat at the traffic lights on the new Datça road when I noticed that my passenger side mirror was still turned in from parking earlier. I reached over to pop it back into place and BAM - right there and then, to the tune of 'Super Massive Black Hole' by Muse, on the seat of my new car; my mother fucking waters broke.

I had no idea what to do, and my brain didn't seem to be functioning properly either as I remember being more concerned that I couldn't quite reach my mirror to pop it into place than my waters breaking...!

I snapped out of it when I was deafened by cars and other vehicles hooting and a tooting at me, as daft lass here was sat in a daze with the lights on green.
Then I stalled Suzette the Swift.
Oh the shame.

After pulling myself together I made a snap decision to drive directly to Barış's work, which thankfully, was not a million miles away.

As soon as I arrived I called him to come out. I didn't think I needed to tell him why because the urgency in my voice surely would have given the game away, after all, I never just drop by his work...

While waiting, I got up out of the car to see what devastation I had caused the seat. Bad move because a second burst of waters soaked what was left dry!
I was a dripping fucking mess but all I could worry about was if these 'ere minge waters would cause my car seat to grow mushrooms.

See, head totally not in the game...

Bariş eventually sauntered out of his office, clocked the state of me and said 'Lei, I think you've had an accident'.
Dumb-ass.
Mind you, I don't blame him for thinking as much, it's not the first time I've pissed myself, but come on, did I look like I'd just had an uncontrollable laughing fit FFS?

I explained what was happening and the sheer look of terror that crept across his face *should* have alerted me for just what was to come. Alas, it didn't.

He bolted inside to tell his boss that he was leaving, while I called the Gynae.

Good ole Gynae, always the clever cunt when he informed me that I *may* be in labour and to come on down to the hospital to get checked over.

May be in labour? Seriously, when one has burst a leak that can only be described as a gushing American style fire hydrant, there is no two ways about it mate – the baby that had been living inside me for the last 9 months was on her way out, come hell or minging mushroom water!

But wait; I hadn't shaved the ludicrous mess of a lady garden because I was saving that tedious task for Monday - Fuck sake! The thought did cross my mind to quickly go home and shave the rainforest because a beautiful rainforest it was not, but Bariş was having none of it.
Swine.
I needn't have worried as the midwives went on to dry shave my area (ouchieeeee!) and fuck it all up with the patchiest job I have ever seen, all the while passing knowing glances to each other...
Come on, I was 11 days early!

Anyway, with Barış now ready to leave work, we were good to go, and as he doesn't have a car licence, I had to drive myself to bloody hospital, sodden seat and all.

Arriving at the hospital we looked like a circus act what with Barış running around flapping his arms like an armadillo desperate to take flight, and me dancing all over the hospital floor due to my ever-leaking toot causing my flip flops to slip and slide all over! Honestly, what a state.
Not quite how I pictured arriving to give birth, that's 'fo sho...

While Barış checked me in at the front desk, I made my way upstairs to the midwives to be checked over. All looked well they said, but I wasn't allowed home to get my stuff, so I had to send Barış instead. The problem was my case was only half packed as I hadn't been expecting this to happen on a mundane Friday afternoon, nearly 2 weeks earlier than expected. That'll teach me for not being more organised as my poor little Lennie had to leave the hospital drowned in clothes for a 6 to 9-month-old.
Bloody Barış never could follow directions well...

Anyway, the midwives told me that now was the time to relax so rolled me into my private room and subsequently buggered off. As I hadn't started my contractions yet and was in no pain, I called various people to let them know the score, my parents included. Unless I was in for a four-day labour, they were definitely not going to make it in time. So, I did what any freaked-out girl could and called in the bestie.

Kimmy is literally the most reliable person ever in emergencies as she is cool, calm and collect. I suppose that's why she's in the position that she's in while I'm still bobbing around looking for my life purpose.
Anyway, I told her the situ and 1.5 hours later she was at my bedside. Not bad considering she was closing up resort for the season. Oh, and that resort was Fethiye!
What is usually a 2-hour drive, she made in less than half the time.

Yup, you can always count on your Minger.

Before the contractions began, we had about an hour of chill time. It wasn't bad to begin with; I took it quite well and was still pigging out on goodies and treats that both Barış and Kimmy had brought in.
The good times didn't last though and after the monitor started to show that my contractions were hitting 30 (in whichever unit they are measured in), I demanded the drugs.
The powers that be had other ideas and didn't want to give them up because I wasn't 5cm dilated. I was, in fact, only 1cm.
It took me 2 hours of constant moaning plus forcing Barış and Kimmy on rotation to beg the midwives, and, after an unexpected enema, I finally got my first epidural at 3cm dilated.
Oh happy days - life was good again.

And so, I sat back in joy and watched the monitor shoot up to over 100 and laughed in the face of pain.
Epidural, you absolute beaut you.

But then it went wrong, terribly wrong...

THINGS NO ONE TELLS YOU ABOUT LABOUR

Apparently, epidurals don't always work:

After 1.5 hours of loving life from the first hit of the good stuff, the pain returned. I informed the midwife, and after a little time, they hooked me up with another dose, set to last another 1.5 hours.

It never kicked in.

Let me repeat that: IT. NEVER. KICKED. IN.

I screamed out in agony every 1.5 minutes each and every time a new contraction hit, and that's the way I remained right the way through till my little ray of painful sunshine greeted us with her presence at 09.55am the following morning.

FYI, I had 6 epidurals in total and only the first fucker worked.

Oh, and to be clear here, there was no gas and air on offer. I went through the whole God damn ordeal stone cold sober.

Gynae's know nothing but at the same time know everything:

My Gynae is a card. He has, what you would call, an odd sense of humour; not bad, just odd. He proved this every time he checked over my area by cracking a joke to ease the tension.
His jokes are not what I would consider appropriate for the run of the mill female in labour, especially when his head is looking up a snatch - so it's a jolly good thing I'm not in the run of the mill club then isn't it?!
Let's put it this way, when being informed that one's area has looked the best that it will ever look, and from this point onwards it's going to resemble porridge, then goes on to ask if Husbando enjoys porridge - I can see why some may take offence, can't you?

Yup, good ole Gynae would fit right in at the cunts club.
And by cunts club, I mean the club I'm part of, not his daily job.
Although...

Other than his random jokes, what really stuck out during my 18-hour hell was his 'push speech'.
When I was 9cm dilated at 08.30am on that eventful Saturday morning, the midwives walked my exhausted arse into the delivery room and hoisted me up onto the push seat.
Whilst my legs were getting strapped down (?), the Gynae went on to deliver the following words:
'This is going to be hard Lei. In fact, this is going to be the hardest thing that you have ever done or will ever do. Your baby is not quite in position, so you are going to have to push extra hard and it's already hard enough - so you're going to have to give it all you've got. I don't want to hear you say you can't do it or you're too tired, and I don't want to listen to you complaining that it hurts. All I want from you is compliance. And when I say push, you push. Understand?'

I nodded, wondering what fresh hell he could possibly be prepping me for?

And then it began.

Without so much as letting me get comfortable, he screamed 'puuussshhhh, pussshhhhhhh' at me every 60 seconds. I was pushing with all my might, but it wasn't good enough for that mad mother fucker - no, he wanted more, more that I simply didn't have to give. Maybe if the epidurals had worked I might have been better at this shit, but they didn't, and I wasn't, and so, he brought out the big guns.

Help was on its way - Hallelujah!

I noticed from the corner of my tear stained eye a big burly midwife heading in my direction. What she did next will haunt me till the end of days.

The scag proceeded to place both her forearms at the top of my stomach and push down so hard that I thought my belly was going to explode.
I nearly burst a fucking blood vessel trying to kick, punch and head butt the vicious mo fo off me.

Strap me in is it? Fuckers.

Fuck my life I had never felt pain like it and I vowed there and then that I would hunt her down and do her in.

I swear to God that all-knowing fucker, let's call her Midwife Trunchbull, seemed to understand the vow I had just made and went on to repeat the performance, and, as if to teach me a lesson, applied double the pressure!

With sheer adrenaline coursing through my veins, I broke free from my binds and fought my way off the delivery seat telling ole Gynae that he could fuck himself, that I was not going through with it, and that Lennie could live in there forever for all I cared.
I would simply be known as the woman that carried her baby through to adulthood, and I was good with that, really I was.

Alas, it was not to be.

I was forced back on to the seat and told in no uncertain terms to grow a pair because it wasn't as painful as I was making out.

Know the feeling of childbirth do you *male* Gynae?

At least he promised not to let Midwife Trunchbull back on my case...

But that then left *him* asking *me* how we planned on getting Lennie out.
Urm, I'm no Doctor, but couldn't he just cut her out? Apparently, that ship sailed about an hour previous, so no. I asked if she could be sucked out instead, and to my sheer delight, the answer was yes!

He went away and a moment later came back with some sort of contraption that was going to save the day – a baby vacuum! He attached that bad boy onto Lennie's head, and, with me pushing with all my might, the vacuum sucking, and a lot of grimacing from ole Gynae, Lennie's head popped out, thankfully followed by her body!

Yippee ki-yay mother fucker – my job was done!

When they placed Lennie on top of me, her body all white and slimy, my first thought was how gross that they didn't clean her up a bit before giving her to me.

Let me ask you this: Who the hell thinks such shit after just giving birth?

I had just pushed a brand new human out of my flange, and instead of being all filled with wonder, I was consumed with OCD.
Typical bloody Lei.
But then she opened her teeny tiny brand-new eyes and looked at me. It was like a lightning bolt and I no longer gave a damn that little Lennie was leaving slug like marks up my sopping wet pyjama top. Not much anyway.

Those baby blues did not make me forget the pain (then or now), but they did make me feel like it was all worthwhile.
Sort of.
Mind you, the rush of love that everyone talks about didn't happen right then, that happened days later when Lennie wasn't even with me - but I will get to that later.

With Lennie still on top of me, I could feel more tugging going on down in my nether region.
I looked down and saw that Gynae had hold of a bit of old rope and was moving it from side to side around the general direction of my fairy. What the hell was that sneaky fucker up to now, and why did he have rope up my gash?

That rope turned out to be my umbilical cord and he was tugging on it to deliver the placenta.

Seriously, why didn't I do my research before going through this shit?

Once the placenta was firmly out and in one piece, Gynae turned to me with a glint in his eye and said "Now Lei, you're not one of these new age hippies that wants to eat this thing are you?" No Gynae, I could safely say not, and - eww gross!

And with that, he stitched me up, ignoring all pleas to stich the whole damn thing up, because that, 'Dear Diary', is forever more closed for business…
Word.

Chocolate tea pots have never much amused me:

For the duration of labour Barış was in one of two positions:
Position 1) His head in his hands rocking back and forth
Position 2) Asleep

That fucker was neither use nor ornament for the entire ordeal and Kimmy had to ban him from the room on various occasions for fear that his presence would tip me over the edge.
And, he was not in the room when his daughter was born either. Had he of seen what went on there, I 100% believe he would be 10 feet under by now...

He also wasn't particularly useful after the birth, and on night one of Lennie's arrival, I really needed the help.
I was physically and mentally exhausted, plus I couldn't go to the loo without hitting the deck. So I asked Barış to help with my toilet visits and Lennie's feeds so I could get some rest – after all – he'd had a full night of shut eye and was perfectly refreshed.

Alas, as fate would have it, life had other ideas.

Barış went on to contract a "sickness" that had the doctors swarming round him like *he* was the one that had just given birth.
Poor ole battered bajingo over here consequently had to ask for a bed pan as I simply knew from that point on that I would not be getting any help going to the lav, nor with the feeding of little Lennie.
And lucky me, this "sickness" went on to last 6 fucking days with daily trips to the hospital for injections and sympathy...
During those 6 days Barış *couldn't* do a bloody thing.
And on day 7 he went back to work.

Until now, I never realised I had cunt tattooed on my fod. Must remember to get that removed ASAP – because as much of a cunt as Lei frikkin' Lawson is, one simply does not want it on ones fod!

So just what was this mystery "sickness" that turned my Husbando into a quivering wreck?

You will never believe it, but the doctors told him they believed it to be psychological, probably caused by the trauma of seeing me in so much pain.

Let's look at that again shall we: A psychological illness caused from seeing *me* in pain.

Jesus effing Christ, I just went through the most harrowing experience of my whole entire life, feeling pain like nothing else before, and this fucker goes and gets a pissing psychological illness from doing nothing else other than watching me!

What's wrong with this picture...?

And then, life began:

So, I was basically left with this cute little baby that I had no idea what to do with. Yup, it's fair to say that I found myself totally unprepared.
At home I had no baby gear other than the basics: clothes, nappies and milk - but that's where it ended.
How on earth did I think the nursery was ready?
Honestly, how?!

Had I have known that a baby swing was an absolute essential, I would have had that thing rigged up ready for our arrival to escape the tedious cries of an overtired baby. And had I have known that wind could cause my little darling so much pain, I would have had gas drops bought by the dozen.
Ahh, hindsight - such a wonderful thing…

I really should have done my homework instead of pissing around getting my winter wardrobe out from under the bed. I mean imagine walking into a nursery that has fuck all in it? What the bloody hell was I thinking? Probably that the nursery fairies were just going to show up and take care of it all…
Stupid stupid stupid me.

Yes, I can honestly say that my baby planning was very ill-considered. Mum says I'll know better for next time. But I can assure you there will be no next time. No, not ever.
And, just to prove this fact, I'm sending Barış to get 'done'.

The *one* thing that was well thought out was that I would not be offering up the boob.

Oh, how the paediatrician had a fit about this, but, I have never been a gal that lets bullies win. My God, his incessant demands were never ending! He Mum shamed me at every opportunity available: in front of Kimmy, whilst I was alone, and to Husbando personally - but each and every time, the answer was the same – NO BLOODY BOOBIES.

That mo fo nearly got a smack in the gob on his last-ditch attempt. I was sick of his bully boy tactics by then, way past exhausted, and in no mood to take any man's shit, especially not this man, so he found himself kicked out of my private room with a flea in his ear and warned never to ask again...

He did though, on a follow up visit.
Cunt.

Of course I know I'm in the minority, but I simply couldn't face it. My nipples cringe at the thought of Barış going near them let alone a hungry little baby that will sprout teeth soon.
No siree, breast feeding is not for me.

You may wonder if I've come to regret my decision now that baby Lennie is here?
I can say with all honesty, that no I haven't.
Lennie is a perfectly healthy chubby cheeked baby who is constantly starving and is now on hungry baby milk. Had she of been swinging off a tit I think she would have permanently scarred my nips seeing the way she attacks each and every bottle.

So no, I do not regret my decision.
And my nips have remained intact and eternally grateful.

THINGS THEY DON'T TELL YOU ABOUT AFTER THE BIRTH

The Halo:

Once firmly ensconced at home (and away from the prying eyes of nasty paediatricians), I decided to check my baby over to make sure she had all her fingers and toes, two ears and a nose - something that I hadn't done in hospital because it simply didn't cross my mind. Thankfully everything was where it should be - but wait, what was this on her head?
Was it the sign I had been looking for?

Praise be, Lennie Mai really is our saviour - she has a frikkin' halo!

Oh wait no, that's just the mark the vacuum made when sucking the poor little bugger out.

No one told me that my dear sweet angel would be scarred; I was not mentally prepared for that! But thankfully, after 2 weeks it had totally cleared, and I was left with a perfect little head that screams for fun.

The Recovery:

The reason I didn't choose my most preferable pain free method of child birth (a caesarean) was because I was told that the recovery time would be a lot longer than having a natural birth. Whoever told me that deserves to be shot. Not just because I had the birth from hell, but because my recovery was just as long as a caesarean, if not longer!

OK, so I could pick Lennie up, feed and change her, but I couldn't sit, stand or sleep - all due to the throbbing going on "down there". It was a constant reminder to the hell I'd been through and subsequently caused flash backs.
Not to mention I had to wear adult nappies for the first 3 weeks, and still now, I'm wearing brick like fanny pads because I bleed like a satanic creature from the depths of hell.
Yup, no one told me about the eternal period that would bestow me. One more homework blunder on my part…

Another little bathroom surprise was what I found in my adult nappies on more than one occasion – let's just say that if I wasn't vegetarian, I would never eat chopped liver or jelly ever again!

And don't get me started about blowing ones' nose!
Shit the bed, if I've pissed myself once, I've pissed myself 100 times these last two and a half months! I swear I never thought I would have piss running down my legs in the most inappropriate of situations, like slap bang in the middle of Carrefour – but, piss happens!

And while we are on the subject of "down there", I believe Husbando may have lost the friggin' plot when asking for some nookie!
WT Actual Fuck man???
The only way I can describe my toot is like road kill, and that's being kind. Oh, and porridge.
Thank God for small mercies because Barış can't stand porridge…
#Justfuckoff.

M-I-L's – Who'd 'av 'em?:

So the day I got out of hospital was the day my Mother in law arrived for her first visit. As soon as Barış called to tell her Lennie had landed, she was here like shit off a shovel. In fact, she was waiting on our doorstep by the time we arrived home from hospital.

In some ways she was a big help, especially as my own olds hadn't arrived yet, and what with Barış and his invisible illness rendering him unable to lift a fork to his own mouth, I welcomed the assistance.

But in other ways, well, not so much:
Example 1) Instead of helping me with the general running of the house, she waited hand and foot on Barış.
Not me.
Just Barış.

Example 2) I couldn't stand for long in the kitchen due to my smashed pasty, so you would think she would have offered to cook right?
Urm, no.
On day 2 of Lennie, me and my porridge muff had to stand in the kitchen making sandwiches for *them* to scoff while they got to do the fun stuff and gaze at *my* little baby while she slept.
I couldn't eat *my* sarnie as when it came to me sitting down for a bite, Lennie kicked off, and as no one offered to feed the baby, well, I didn't get fed.
Out of spite I threw my butty in the bin.
What a cunt.
And by cunt, I mean me.

Example 3) On the flip side, when M-I-L didn't require feeding, any time Lennie made a squeak she would rush over, have her up and out of the Moses basket with a bottle in her mouth before I could say boo to a goose. And should I get the chance to feed my own baby, she would grab her off me every time she coughed!
Talk about boundaries, or lack thereof!!

I assumed she would leave when my olds arrived two days later, but, that didn't happen.
What is it they say about assuming? It makes an ass out of you and me.
But only me.
Quite.

She stayed for a further 8 days, sleeping in the nursery, meaning I couldn't use my nursery and had to do all things baby in my bedroom.
Colour me not impressed.

I'm not ashamed to admit that I breathed a massive sigh of relief when she finally did leave. Alas, it was short lived.
I could have killed Bariş and his big gob when he let slip that my olds had moved into their own apartment for the rest of their stay, giving M-I-L the green light to visit again, and this time, bring people!
Yup, a month later she was back, this time bringing with her Bariş's brother, his wife and toddler!

They planned to stay for 2 weeks but ended up staying 4 days, which was 4 days too long when you are sleep deprived and in desperate need of a shower, and every time you think about taking said shower, one of the family members always seemed to have just got out and used up all the hot water!

And it didn't help that M-I-L and wifey hate dogs and squealed every time Gucci came near them or the toddler, waking Lennie in the process.
FML they were like a tag team bending Bariş's ear to get rid of *'the dog'*.

Ha! As if!

This is Gucci's house when all said and done, and Gucci is still my first born.

Although, during Lennie and Gucci's first introduction, Guch very nearly swallowed her foot whole, and I'm not afraid to say that I

panicked. For one small moment, I wondered just what I would do if Gucci decided he didn't want a little sister? After all, I have been *his* Mummy alone for the last 12 years…
Thank the good lord above that I didn't have to wonder again, because when I snapped out of my daze and turned around, I found Barış grinning from ear to ear holding Gucci while he enthusiastically licked Lennie's little foot, all the while Lennie slept on, unbeknown to her that she has a big brother just waiting for her to be old enough to play with…

Sorry, I digressed - anyway, I was scarily close to snapping point when I informed Barış that it was either them or me when he politely asked them to leave.
Now I know I don't speak Turkish and all, but I swear Barış said something along the lines of 'foreigners are not like us, they hate their family and won't let them stay in the house'… And do you know what? I didn't even mind that he used me as an excuse. Fuck it, they were leaving and that's all I cared about.

Off you fuck unwanted house guests – off you fuck.

Sleep is underrated:

As my insomniac Mum has previously informed me; sleep deprivation is dangerous.
I've never had to worry about it before as I can sleep literally anywhere, however, I am now starting to understand just exactly what she meant...

I knew of course I would experience sleepless nights, but I don't think I really grasped what that meant. In all honestly, I believed I would have a super sleeper that slept straight through from the get-go.
I don't.
I feel that I may have been lulled into a false sense of security (or I'm just plain stupid) in believing Kat when she told me that night feeds would be a 5-minute job and I would be able to drift straight off once done...
Lennie's night feeds are nothing of the sort and last a good half hour each time because a night guzzler she is not, and then of course there is a nappy change to get through, and soothing her back off to sleep – all of which takes somewhere in the region of 50 mins each and every time.
And no, I never can drift straight back off because I am up checking on Lennie's breathing at least twice more before the brain finally gives itself up to exhaustion...

Yup, my wannabe sloth had me up 3 times a night every 2 hours right through till just recently when she started sleeping for longer periods. And by longer periods, I mean she occasionally sleeps for 3 hours straight.

This one night when M-I-L was here on her second visit, I was that sleep deprived that at 4am while rushing to warm Lennie's bottle, instead of pouring the boiled kettle water into Lennie's bottle warmer, I poured it all over my arm instead.
Jesus fuck did I scream.
Bariş looked alarmed as he had never before heard me string as many swear words together at one time as I did right then, and, just to be

polite, I translated each and every one so that M-I-L (who had come out of her room during the commotion) could also understand.

See, I know what counts when it comes to speaking Turkish.

So, to sum it up, I have now mastered the art of sleeping standing up because when large noticeable marks are left on one's body that are neither unidentified booze bruises, nor sex marks, it makes one look like some sort of battered wife.
And FFS, that's the not a good look for a new Mum to have...!

Anyone for a Muffin?:

I knew that my body wouldn't resemble its former self as soon as I'd popped, but what I didn't expect was what was left in its place.
My poor ole stomach looked like a deflated balloon, and that's how it stayed for a month and a half.

Mum couldn't believe it when she clapped eyes on me, and when she asked if I had another baby up there that they forgot, I won't lie when I tell you that I saw red. I mean, wouldn't you?

Had she forgotten what it was like after giving birth because I can't ever imagine forgetting what my tummy looked like then?
But no, she hadn't forgotten, it simply hadn't happened to her. She went on to inform me that she was the thinnest she had ever been after spawning me, so couldn't quite figure out how it had gone so terribly wrong *for* me.
That's nice isn't it?

So, in an effort to combat my additional weight, I decided to give my magic coffee a go. Mind you, I didn't have that much extra weight considering the size of my stomach, only 2 and a half
kilos to my pre-pregnant self - but I did want rid of the bulge that ruined every outfit and stopped me fitting into my skinny jeans.
And it would have worked too had my parents not been here for 2.5 stinkin' months, feeding me up at every possible turn, consequently turning me into the very 'healthy' 69.5 Kilos that I find myself today, ready to slit my wrists.

Now they have gone and the coffee has run dry, I have started to eat normally again in the hopes that the weight comes off by itself because the last thing I want to do is start a diet, or god forbid, *exercise*. Oh hell's to the no, fuck that shit, I barely find time to heat up 3 minute pasta let alone cook for a bloody diet!

My trainer friend Julia told me she would send me some gentle tummy exercises to start once I was 3 months post birth. She said she wanted to be sure that my uterus had gone back into place before starting anything, and she would be right to wait too because this morning when I blew my nose, I pissed myself.

Thanks uterus, you have reminded me that kegal's should be a way of life.

So, basically…

The after birth has been no party. In fact, it has been a rather up and down period in my life. The lack of sleep, the Mum shame, the worry that I'm not looking after Lennie properly - the list is endless. But then she started smiling and FML that takes away all the shit immediately.

Of course we have good days, and then, some not so good days, but it evens itself out. The only real issue I've had so far is dressing her correctly.
Does she really need ten ton of clothing like M-I-L had her trussed up in?
I doubt it.

Me and *my* Mum dressed her in what we thought was appropriate for the weather, which at the time was a rather warm 25 degrees. We had a hat in the baby bag but didn't feel the need to put it on as it was so hot outdoors. What we didn't expect was to be told off by the cashier whilst paying for our shopping in the new 'Carrefour'! Shocking.com

And, as we were only going shopping and not *out* out, I hadn't bothered to dress her in her Sunday best. She was under a light cloth blanket anyway, and, because I didn't fancy being bollocked again for not having a hat on my baby, I had also thrown a muslin over the front of the pram (but not so that she could cook in the pram).
But, I didn't bank on bumping smack bang into Larissa and two of her gormless gang members, dressed like they were heading to prom night now did I…

Larissa, desperate for a coo at baby Lennie, opened up the muslin, grinned like a Cheshire cat and said "Lei, you look like you come from a poor family using socks as mittens for your lovely baby, what's wrong with you?"

Oh fuckity fuck, why didn't I just put mittens on her when leaving the house?

But, for once, my mind was clear as a bell, and I retorted with "Why don't you just fuck off you nasty northern troll - I live in the real world, and in this real world I now have a million and one things to do, and sometimes forget to put Lennie's mittens on. Does she look bothered that she's wearing socks as mittens? No. You're the only fucker that's bothered, so why don't you just jog on, cunt".

I then turned on my flip flop's leaving her open mouthed and red faced, trotted out into the sunny car park, hopped into my new car and drove off into the sunset, accidentally leaving behind the shopping, Lennie, plus Mum and Dad.

I made it half way home before I realised.
#WhataTit

But I had finally told that twat where to go leaving her speechless, and really, I couldn't be any bloody happier. I wish of course that I had done it long since, however, I hadn't reached the end of my tether *then*.
There will be repercussions I'm sure, but I no longer feel the need to sweat the small stuff. My life just got a whole lot bigger and the only thing I need to sweat is making sure that Lennie is well cared for...

A fine example of excellent caring happened last night when Lennie got her first cold.
After watching a YouTube video, I proceeded to suck the snot right out of each dainty little nostril using a snot sucking device.
Now there's a sentence I would never have believed could be real had I not had to do it myself...
I was physically sick half way through the job, but after wiping my gob I pulled up my 'Bridget Jones's' and carried on.

See, I'm doing OK. Some of the time.

And so, I take you back to that rush of love.
It was day 7 of little Lennie's life and I was waiting for my olds in the parking lot of Migros while they shopped. I was sat in the car because my fanny couldn't endure the pain of standing any longer,

and whilst I waited, I played Lennie's song on my phone – 'Lenny' by Stevie Ray Vaughn.

Right there, in said parking lot, with people walking by going about their business, I burst out crying.

That's when the rush of love hit and my earlier vow to hunt Midwife Trunchbull down and do her in disappeared as a new one took its place. I promised to never let the world hurt little Lennie. I promised to do my very best for her, to bring her up to be a strong female, one that would take no shit and to one day rule the world.

I'm going to make you cringe now, but I think I think I may, just may, have found my purpose in life.

Now there's a turn up for the fucking books...

Who would have thought that back in 2011 when writing my first diary that I would be sat here now writing this?

Not fucking me pal.

But I tell ya what, I think it was meant to be.

And with that, Mummy Lei, Mother of prophet Lennie Mai was born.

Boom!

And now, 'Dear Diary', it's about time that I bid you adieu. I do, after all, have bottles to make, because I'm a Mum and that's what Mums do.

Some of us drink too, especially if your part of my club, and you know the one I mean ;)

Wishing you love and light and a good night's sleep,

Lei

(and Lennie Mai, the first-born Gucci and not forgetting El Husbando Barış)

To be continued?

I doubt it, but stranger things have happened.

MADE IN MARMARIS

ABOUT THE AUTHOR

Louise Bell lives in Marmaris / Turkey and has done since the sweet age of 16. She is an ex rep, has a dog called Gucci and is married to a Turkish chap named Mehmet. They recently welcomed a new addition to the family (and a little sister for Gucci), Lola Rose. Although Louise wanted to name her Lennie, she was over-ruled by Mehmet.

Louise is one of the more positive people that belong to this world and enjoys a glass of vodka, whisky and pink gin from time to time, although these days, sipping a cup of strong coffee is much more her favorite tipple because hangovers and babies don't mix.

Connect with Louise:

Join my Facebook page: www.facebook.com/TheMarmarisDiaries

Subscribe to my newsletter: www.louisebell.weebly.com

PLEA FROM THE AUTHOR:

Hello fellow Marmaris lover! So you have got to the end of my book - I hope that means you enjoyed it? Whether or not you did, I would just like to thank you for giving me your valuable time to try and entertain you. Thank you for giving my book a chance and for spending your hard earned cash on it. For that I am eternally grateful.

If you enjoyed this book and would like to help, then you could think about leaving a review on Amazon, Goodreads, or anywhere else that readers visit. The most important part of how well a book sells is how many positive reviews it has, so if you leave me one then you are directly helping me to continue on this road as a writer.

Thank you in advance if you do, you are helping out an aging rock star in what has been a lifelong dream :)

Printed in Great Britain
by Amazon

21260939R00078